LAURIE

707.337.6791

plezse return ♡

A PERFECT SCORE

A PERFECT SCORE

THE ART, SOUL, AND BUSINESS OF A 21ST-CENTURY WINERY

CRAIG AND KATHRYN HALL

CENTER
STREET

NEW YORK   BOSTON   NASHVILLE

Copyright © 2016 by Kathryn Hall and Craig Hall

Cover design by Jamie Chandler and Justine Di Fede
Photographer: John Bedell
Cover copyright © 2016 by Hachette Book Group, Inc.

Hachette Book Group supports the right to free expression and the value of copyright. The purpose of copyright is to encourage writers and artists to produce the creative works that enrich our culture.

The scanning, uploading, and distribution of this book without permission is a theft of the author's intellectual property. If you would like permission to use material from the book (other than for review purposes), please contact permissions@hbgusa.com. Thank you for your support of the author's rights.

Center Street
Hachette Book Group
1290 Avenue of the Americas
New York, NY 10104
centerstreet.com
twitter.com/centerstreet

First Hardcover Edition: September 2016

Center Street is a division of Hachette Book Group, Inc.
The Center Street name and logo are trademarks of Hachette Book Group, Inc.

The publisher is not responsible for websites (or their content) that are not owned by the publisher.

The Hachette Speakers Bureau provides a wide range of authors for speaking events. To find out more, go to www.HachetteSpeakersBureau.com or call (866) 376-6591.

Library of Congress Cataloging-in-Publication Data

Names: Hall, Craig, 1950– author. | Hall, Kathryn, 1947– author.
Title: A perfect score : the art, soul, and business of a 21st century winery / Craig and Kathryn Hall.
Description: New York : Center Street, [2016]
Identifiers: LCCN 2016015454| ISBN 978-1-4555-3576-7 (hardcover) | ISBN 978-1-4789-1265-1 (audio download) | ISBN 978-1-4555-3578-1 (ebook)
Subjects: LCSH: Wine and wine making. | Wineries.
Classification: LCC TP548 .H2235 2016 | DDC 641.2/2—dc23 LC record available at https://lccn.loc.gov/2016015454

ISBNs: 978-1-4555-3576-7 (hardcover), 978-1-4555-3578-1 (ebook)

Printed in the United States of America

RRD-C

10 9 8 7 6 5 4 3 2

To the Bobs who shaped our Napa Valley journey:
Bob Walt, Kathryn's father, whose contagious love of the land
brought him, his wife, Dolores, and their children to the wine
country, and thereby us to Napa Valley
and
Bob Mondavi, who with his wife, Margrit, made us feel welcome
before we arrived, supported once we were here, and increasingly
inspired as the years pass by.

CONTENTS

CONTENTS

Meet Little Bunny Foo Foo

Napa Valley's countryside is full of rabbits. They're everywhere. Stand in any vineyard for 30 minutes and you're sure to see several bouncing through the vines. There's one rabbit, however, that you can see without even getting out of your car: ours. His name is Bunny Foo Foo. He was built in China, shipped across the sea, and assembled with the help of two very large cranes. Our BFF is 35 feet long and 27 feet high, suspended mid-hop on one foot above our St. Helena vineyard bordering Highway 29, the artery that connects San Francisco to Napa Valley's heavenly wine country.

Bunny Foo Foo has a coat of stainless steel that sparkles madly as it reflects our brilliant California sun. We love watching cars pull to the side of the road as people smile at and photograph the sculpture's exuberance. Most visitors think of our rabbit as simply a particularly bold—and, for some, controversial—piece of contemporary art. For us, Bunny Foo Foo is much more. He embodies the Napa Valley we know, love, and have labored in since 1995.

We wanted a rabbit at our St. Helena property because it reminds us of Kathryn's grape-growing roots. As soon as the kids were old enough to walk, one of Kathryn's rituals was to lead them through her parents' Mendocino County vineyard, singing their family wine-country-themed version of the children's song: *Little Bunny Foo Foo hopping through the vineyard, scooping up the field mice and bopping them on the head.* By the time we bought our own land in the Napa Valley in 1995, the kids were too old to be sung to (voluntarily, that is), but the bunny sculpture remains symbolic of that special time.

Bunny Foo Foo is first and foremost a stunning piece of art, the work of Lawrence Argent, the brilliant Australian sculptor who now lives in Colorado. Art is a huge part of the Napa Valley experience and a huge part of our lives. It's also particularly central to the way we've envisioned our winery. Since a memorable wine-drinking experience is always about more than just what is in the glass, we've put a lot of effort into assembling an art collection that would enhance the experience of our guests. Bunny Foo Foo is where he is because he captures the imagination and attracts the interest of winery visitors—a crucial part, we believe, of any thriving winery today. Bunny Foo Foo also delivers an unspoken invitation to turn in to our tasting room.

The story of Bunny Foo Foo hasn't been all rainbows and sunshine. Believe us, absolutely no change happens in Napa Valley without controversy. Installing this particular piece of art in such a prominent location was no exception. On the very evening Bunny Foo Foo went up, as we were standing in line at the local Sunshine Market, the checker commented on how much she loved the new sculpture. Before Kathryn (who is normally the more outgoing of the two of us) could open her mouth to answer, the person behind us in line chimed in, "You mean that huge rabbit thing? Well it's certainly *LAAAARGE* enough." We got the message. Later that week the county supervisor began receiving complaints that the county needed to pass an ordinance requiring Bunny Foo Foo be moved. Luckily, Bunny Foo Foo was perfectly legal in every respect, and we're happy to say that since then most everyone has come around and loves him as much as we do.

So, why are we going on and on about our big rabbit sculpture? Because Bunny Foo Foo has come to symbolize our Napa experience, and he sums up in so many different ways the adventures chronicled in this book. When we look at him, we think about the roots we've put down in Napa. He represents the intersection of art, nature, globalization, and technology that we see as being at the heart of the winemaking process. Running a winery is pretty straightforward: You grow the grapes, harvest them, ferment the juice, age the wine, bottle it, and sell it. The difference lies in the approach. Ask 100 people to draw a bunny, and they'll produce 100 very different renditions. The same principle applies here. In our case, our personalities and passions, along with those of our team, have dictated our decisions and shaped everything from the design of our wineries to the taste of the wine itself.

Bunny Foo Foo's presence trumpeting the HALL name to all who drive past also signifies what we see as the future of the wine industry: the importance of building a strong, high-quality brand known for its superior wine and its ability to understand and respond to the needs and desires of our patrons.

Lastly, the controversy over Bunny Foo Foo encapsulates

the strange and particular politics of Napa, where wine-making, environmental concerns, liberal thought, a desire for tourism, a longing to keep the Valley local, and just plain old "I've got mine, so not in my backyard" thinking are all pitted against each other.

Yes, Bunny Foo Foo means *all* that to us and more. But now we're getting ahead of our story.

CHAPTER 1

Bonds of Love and Wine

Spring had hit. Napa Valley's green hills cradled vineyards full of vines beginning to leaf out. The sunny April day had compelled Craig to put down the top on the convertible. Open-air travel allowed him to drink in the blossoming fruit trees and the unruly yellow-flowering mustard enveloping the base of all the gnarled grape trunks.

He made his way down the hill and over to Highway 29, Napa's main thoroughfare and home to wineries that have contributed to the Valley's fame. Domaine Chandon. Robert Mondavi. Heitz. Martini. Beaulieu. Beringer. Charles Krug. Cakebread. The list goes on and on. Unfortunately, that day so did the bumper-to-bumper traffic.

As Craig inched his way toward the small town of St. Helena, located in the heart of Napa Valley, he noticed an old winery with the look of a disheveled, ignored child who never has to take a bath. Craig had probably passed the winery a thousand times without ever paying attention, it being one of those places that seems to compel you to avert your gaze. No one wants to look at a place that feels old, deserted, and sad, especially in Napa where you can get whiplash from trying to take in all the surrounding beauty.

Craig has spent most of his business career turning properties around, so once the old winery caught his eye, it caught his attention as well. Edgewood Estate Winery, as it was known then, was flanked by a little bit of vineyard in front, the ugliest set of warehouse buildings Craig had ever seen in Napa Valley, and what seemed like acres of parking lot with a healthy crop of weeds growing up through old, broken concrete.

As he crawled toward his lunch date at Tra Vigne, Craig continued to stare at the neglected property. When his car stopped directly in front of the winery, he looked over at the industrial warehouses located just behind and to the side of the tasting room for Edgewood and felt an instant sense that we would buy this run-down facility. He saw in that moment what it would become and how we could parlay our passion for making wine into a bold, new adventure. He had no question about any of this. It was meant to be.

After a nice long luncheon and a chance to catch up with some friends, Craig started his journey back home. Traffic moved a little faster than before, but not much. He passed the Harvest Inn and the beautiful Victorian home that is Sutter Home's tasting room, and then there it was. The least attractive parking lot in Napa Valley with the Edgewood tasting room in the middle of a handful of driveways that snaked in and out with no apparent purpose.

He turned in and drove onto the property. When he saw a fenced area that was open (not great security), he headed that direction, trying, with limited success, to avoid the broken glass so he didn't end up with a flat tire. On the other side of the fence he found 59 oversized outdoor production tanks typically used in a high-production/low-value winery. Instead of being housed in an enclosed tank room, the preferred location when making high-quality wine, these outdoor, exposed tanks stood sentry in a long row along the back of the property, each rising 30 feet atop concrete bases that added another 5 feet in height.

This place seemed like nothing else in Napa. It just didn't fit. Although Napa started out as a rural community and was better known in the 1960s for housing a state mental hospital than for growing grapes, over its 150-year history it has evolved into a region famous for premium wines and stunning wineries designed to make visitors want to linger and enjoy. Despite Napa Valley's worldwide renown, this growing area accounts for just 4 percent of all the wines made in California and a mere 0.4 percent of the world's wines. More than half of the wineries belonging to the Napa Valley Vintners trade organization make fewer than 5,000 cases of wine a year. Only one out of every five Napa wineries makes more than 10,000 cases of wine annually. This winery, this *wine factory* to be more precise, looked like it could produce a hundred times that much, and all of it bulk rather than quality wine.

The huge tanks were covered with a dirty, whitish-gray, foamy-looking material designed to shield them from the outdoor temperature changes. A metal framework of stairs rose up the south side of the lineup and connected to a series of catwalks that ran along the tops of the tanks. With the exception of the large wooden warehouse that faced Highway 29, the place looked like an unsightly maze of concrete and metal surrounded by even more cracked cement studded with weeds—a no-man's land, deserted, unattended, and ignored.

The largest structure on the property, a warehouse with a

rounded top like an old World War II Quonset hut but ten times the size, housed the wine barrels. Even to an untrained eye, the warehouse looked like it would implode at any minute. Here and there, vines had overtaken parts of the structure, as if nature was mercifully trying to hide it.

CRAIG

I was just beginning to gain a little experience in the world of how wine is made and what a winery should look like. I knew this wasn't it. Edgewood, as it was called on the sign in front, was by far the biggest winery I had ever seen. I would quickly learn that at one point in its history, it had functioned as the Napa Valley Cooperative, producing an estimated 40 percent of Napa Valley's wines in the late 1930s. By 1955, due to a contract with Ernest and Julio Gallo, who agreed to buy every drop it produced, the Napa Valley Cooperative Winery was close to operating at its capacity, making over one million cases of wine. The Gallo brothers then labeled the bulk wine and marketed it as their own.

But that was then. When I stumbled upon the old Napa Valley Co-op on that spring day in 2003, it seemed like a lot of the facility was unoccupied. Although I did eventually find out that the facility was making a little wine, it wasn't anywhere close to high volume. I was clearly looking at a mismanaged asset that was just awful. In fact, if I had lived behind or to the side of it, I would have been pretty upset. All that noisy outdoor winemaking equipment and lighting must have made life pretty miserable for the winery's neighbors. At least that's what I thought at the time.

Every passing minute confirmed what I had recognized about the property two hours earlier. Up until this point, we had focused on making small-batch, high-quality wine. This would definitely expand our platform and take our passion for winemaking in a new direction. Even so, in my heart of hearts I knew that Kathy and I would buy this property. I just didn't know why, or who owned it, or even if it was for sale.

Craig had fallen for the wine business even though his background did not include wine. His parents hadn't exactly been teetotalers, but they never drank wine. They kept a stocked bar, but didn't drink much of anything from it. As a teenager, Craig had done his share of sampling, pouring himself some vodka or gin and then filling the liquor bottle with water so his parents wouldn't realize anything was missing. They drank so infrequently that they probably wouldn't have known the difference, although over time some of their vodka and gin basically turned to water.

So even if he had wanted to experiment with wine, there was none at home. As a result, Craig had never become a wine drinker. How ironic that he would end up with a woman whose life had almost always revolved around winemaking in one way or another.

Craig and Kathryn met in 1991 when Kathryn, who was running for mayor of Dallas, called Craig and asked to set up an appointment to talk about her campaign.

"Yes, that sounds good," Craig replied. "I'd like to talk about that and more."

What more? Kathryn thought. She wasn't sure what he had in mind, but it sounded good. She had heard from two mutual friends, one being then–Texas governor Ann Richards, that she and Craig should get to know each other. She would later find out that the governor had given Craig the same pitch.

KATHRYN

Craig's office was on the top floor of a building that had his name on it, buried behind two secretaries. His staff seemed to be in awe of him. To me, however, he just seemed darling, with a sweet smile and a shy manner that didn't mesh with how everyone at the office treated him.

One of his secretaries took me to his office where I started my pitch about why I should be mayor.

"I'll contribute the maximum to your campaign and raise more," he said almost immediately.

Hmm. Mission accomplished. That's when he invited me to lunch. Even better, he took me to an Indian restaurant. Think about it: This was Dallas in 1991. Everyone ate steak. I was a California transplant committed to being vegetarian. I didn't even know Dallas had an Indian restaurant.

Lunch was relaxed and comfortable. Forget saving South Dallas for a while; I was really having fun. Before we got to the second bite of naan, I was talking about my family's vineyard in Mendocino and how big a part wine played in my life.

"I don't drink wine," he said.

Deal killer.

"But I'd like to know more."

Promising.

"Is it true rosé is red and white wine mixed together?"

Setback.

"You've never tried any wine I've made," I said.

"I'd like to."

Hmmm, I thought. *I'm in.*

After lunch I went home, dug out a bottle of my wine from the cellar, wrote a note that said he did need to try my wine, and took the bottle and note to his office, leaving both with one of his secretaries.

This is the most forward I have ever been with a guy, I thought. Remember this was 1991.

I expected a call that afternoon. Nothing. Or that night. Again, nothing. *I sure misread the signals,* I thought after about a week. *He seemed to be so interested in me. But he IS contributing to my campaign, so okay.*

Ten days later, about mid-February, I was working late at my law office when the phone rang. It was Craig, wanting to know if I could have dinner that Friday. I later found out that he had been seeing someone else for the prior year and felt compelled to break it off with her before even calling me.

Dinner was just as fun and easy as lunch had been. It was like we had known each other forever, except there was so much to discover. He asked if I wanted to go out the next day.

The following afternoon we walked along Turtle Creek, which ran through a peaceful neighborhood full of flowers and winding trails in the middle of Downtown Dallas, and talked about how we could spend the rest of our lives together. I would say this suddenness was amazing, but it wasn't. It felt totally normal. Our fit was seamless.

The mayoral election came later that fall. I lost. It was devastating.

Even though my political life was a mess, my personal life had never been better. Craig filled my focus and I was already enjoying not seeing myself in the *Dallas Morning News*, where I had been featured at least once a week for more than a year.

I couldn't wait to bring Craig to my family's home and vineyard in Mendocino County. Our first trip came in March 1992. I told him I was heading to California and invited him to join. He offered to buy the tickets. *Wow, what a keeper,* I thought.

We picked up a rental car at the San Francisco airport and drove up Highway 101 on a typically sunny California day. Craig seemed to appreciate it all. When I drive through the wine country I always think and talk about how stunning it is and how much I love it. I don't mean to do this, but over the years friends have pointed out this tendency. This time I purposefully didn't. I wanted to see Craig's reaction and I didn't want to sell.

He doesn't need to know wine as long as he appreciates the beauty of the area, I thought. *And he sure seems to.*

When we finally arrived at my family's vineyard in Redwood Valley, my heart welled up. I always felt safe when I got to the vineyard. This time that sense of security was compounded by so much pride. I was about to show this guy who had become so important to me my most important place on earth.

CRAIG

That trip really taught me how deeply Kathy was rooted in the wine world. Here was this high-powered lawyer who ran for mayor of Dallas, but who loved to walk through the vines and smell the fresh air as it cooled at night. The first morning as we strolled through the vines, the air hot and the sun glistening on the grapes, she explained that the leaves actually help protect the grapes so that they don't turn to raisins.

I never knew that, I thought.

As we kept going, the dirt and the weeds all seemed to mix together.

"That's nature's way of protecting the soil," Kathy said.

She tasted a grape and identified what stage it had reached in its growth cycle. Then she plucked a few more grapes off the vine and offered them to me. They were not quite as sweet as I expected.

"They'll get sweeter as the Brix goes up later in the season, just before harvest," she said.

Brix, I learned, is a way of measuring the grape's sugar content. In fact, tasting grapes to ascertain their sweetness is one of the ways winegrowers decide when to actually harvest the fruit.

"The grape's taste and color all comes from the skin," Kathy added.

She tore a grape apart, pulling the skin off, and asked me to sample the fleshy interior. It tasted a bit like sugar water, with very little flavor. Next I ate a grape with the skin on. What a different sensation! I began to see that this whole area of wine and farming grapes was a lot more interesting and nuanced than I had ever imagined.

With Kathy as my teacher, I was already learning about vineyards and nature. In addition, she introduced me to plain, basic relaxation. There's something so incredibly different about this way of life. As we took our second walk toward the end of what had been a sunbaked day, the lowering temperatures surprised me. In Texas when it's warm during the day, it's generally warm and sticky during the evening. It doesn't cool off like it did at the California vineyard. This was new and different and fabulous. I could understand how it gets into your being. You simply become one with the earth, and suddenly you have to be part of the world of vineyards and wine. No wonder Kathy had made this such an integral part of her life.

Little did we know at that point that we would wind up with our own vineyards, let alone a winery or two in Napa. Craig, who proposed a year and a half later by placing a diamond at the bottom of a glass of champagne, and Kathryn would have been shocked had they known about the trials that lay ahead, and stunned at just how good the wines we eventually produced would be.

We wouldn't even realize how good our wines could be once we started making them. Every winery owner dreams about producing a perfect scoring vintage (a wine made from grapes grown and harvested in the year listed on the label that earns a perfect score of 100 from a wine critic), but it certainly wasn't top of mind in the early 2000s. You just don't usually go from zero to 100. Especially not in just a few challenging years.

CHAPTER 2

Destination Napa

Most people who plant themselves and grow roots in Napa are all about wine. That's certainly true for Kathryn. She came from a family of wine lovers who, for much of her life, owned and worked a vineyard in California's Mendocino County. She can hardly recall a family gathering where wine wasn't served. The young children drank "children's wine"—sugar water with a few drops of wine added—and the teenagers graduated to a small glass of the real stuff. As the years passed, the family vineyard continued to anchor Kathryn. It called to her, even after she had moved out of state.

KATHRYN

During all the years I spent in Texas getting married, having babies in rapid succession, and then getting divorced, I still visited the family property monthly—first to see my family and then, in 1982, to manage the property after my parents' deaths. It was on those regular trips to California that David and Jennifer, my children, also learned to love this life. The oldest,

David, was hardly old enough to walk when we started strolling through the vineyard many times a day. I would have Jennifer in a hip pack as I held David's hand (I was often alone with the kids, probably a sign that my marriage wasn't doing so well). We sang two songs over and over and over. The first: Mr. Rogers's *Some are fancy on the outside, some are fancy on the inside, everybody's fancy, everybody's fine, your body's fancy and so is mine.* And, since we always saw bunnies as we walked, we sang my version of "Little Bunny Foo Foo," substituting the word *vineyard* for *forest.* The kids loved seeing the cute rabbits frolic among the vines, and so did I. Our caretaker at the vineyard was from Oklahoma and loved shooting, cooking, and eating rabbits. Even though they are not good for the vines, I had forbidden that. I am a vegetarian first, vintner second. So we would look for bunnies along with gun shells as we walked. If we found a casing we would take it back to the caretaker and ask why we had found it.

"If we ever find another, you can no longer work for us," I said more than once. Some threats are hard to keep.

In the winter we would wear rubber boots and parkas, in the summer shorts. We walked every row and knew every vine. We would talk about our walks before we arrived in California and after we returned to Texas. And we would always sing our Bunny Foo Foo song.

Over the years as we returned to Mendocino, Craig learned the Bunny Foo Foo song. Truth be told, however, he was underwhelmed when we first drove to the vineyard.

He wasn't crazy about the home Kathryn's parents had lived in. He wasn't crazy about their property on West Road in Ukiah or the area we'd passed getting there. Mendocino seemed downright scruffy to Craig. Nevertheless, on that first trip with Kathryn to California, he managed to fall in love with that special world of vineyards and wine that so moved the woman who would become his wife.

For a decade following her parents' passing, Kathryn ran the family vineyard. Her parents' trust had specified that both she and her brother, Bob, would manage all their property, including the vineyard, for ten years following the death of the last surviving spouse. During that time, since Bob was less interested in taking an active day-to-day role in the estate management, Kathryn assumed the lead. She didn't mind. As the oldest she felt it was her duty to shoulder family responsibilities. Plus she loved visiting the vineyard from Dallas. Over the years, Bob and their sister, Pam, essentially let Kathryn run things as she chose.

In July, 1992, the parental trust dissolved. The siblings discussed how they would split the corpus of the estate. Pam, who was living in France and rarely came back to the U.S., would get cash. Kathryn had assumed that Bob wouldn't want the vineyard either, but by now he was married and things were different. He did want it.

Kathryn loved that land. She loved the memories of her kids there, and before that of her father working in the vineyard. But she loved her brother more. Growing up, they had been very close. Bob had always had her back. She felt she owed him. Of course he should keep the vineyard. She would take a different asset.

Craig, who had been in Kathryn's life just a year and who

had hardly even sipped wine before we met, didn't just agree, he made a pronouncement.

"I support you 100 percent," he said. "Bob takes the vineyard and we'll find our own vineyard, and it will be even better. We'll find the best available vineyard in the United States."

Even though Craig certainly didn't have wine in his blood, and even though he had just emerged from a Chapter 11 reorganization, he knew how important owning a vineyard and making wine was to Kathryn. He knew she could not imagine not being part of the wine world. She was meant for that. So Craig wholeheartedly took on the idea of finding a vineyard, not out of love for wine, but out of love for Kathryn—a gesture that still touches her to this day.

The original plan was to have a vineyard, followed, eventually, by a winery that produced 5,000 to 7,000 cases of very high-quality wine. And not just any wine. In Kathryn's opinion, Cabernet was king.

Where would we go to make that Cabernet Sauvignon? It took just two seconds to decide: Napa Valley, a community at most 30 miles long and five miles wide, inhabited by a population that is as diverse as the setting is beautiful—young families and grandparents, aging former subscribers to the *Whole Earth Catalog* who came to escape the urban scene, and rich folks from the San Francisco area and Silicon Valley who love the lifestyle and their second homes. Napa's residents also include vintners who love to farm the land, who have raised their families here, and who have grown as the wine business and the Valley have become more sophisticated and more expensive. Then there's the Hispanic community of Napa that, like much of the Napa workforce, plays a vital role in the wine industry. They are the laborers in the vineyards and cellars, and they are increasingly present in tasting rooms as well as in management and winery ownership. Some are also the undocumented workers who line up each morning hoping to find day work for cash. Napa is home to wealthy winery owners who can pay to fly in expensive consultants from around the world, as well as pioneering families like the Mondavis, whose name is more famous than the Valley itself.

Napa is also home to some of the world's top Cabernet Sauvignons.

The Cabernet Sauvignon grape's hardy, highly adaptable vines and thick-skinned fruit that resists both frost and mold—along with its full, rich taste—make it one of the most popular selections among growers. Almost every country in the world that grows grapes for wine grows Cabernet Sauvignon grapes. But in Napa Valley, Cabernet reigns supreme among red wine grapes. Not only is it responsible for 40 percent of the Valley's total wine production, it accounts for 55 percent of the region's crop value.

The quintessential Napa Valley Cabernet Sauvignon is dense, opulent, and symphonic, with balance and beauty to the core. What makes Napa Cabernets different from other wines? In a word, it's the *terroir*—those characteristics that include microclimates, elevation, soil composition, and topography (think slope, the direction it faces, which is called *aspect,* and elevation). And you just don't get much better terroir for Cabernet Sauvignon than in Napa.

Take Napa's weather. It doesn't rain much in the summer, which reduces the risk of disease and leads to more consistent vintages. The days are hot, and the nights are cool and often foggy, which allows the grapes to ripen at a leisurely, even pace as they develop a balanced sugar and acid composition.

Next consider Napa's soil. Actually, make that soils, since there are more than 100 different kinds in this small valley. Volcanic activity and the mountains that flank the Valley to the west and the east, coupled with regular flooding of the Napa River and the fact that San Pablo Bay once reached as far as the site of present-day Yountville, produced this extensive array of soils. The result? As the Napa Valley Vintners website says, "Great wines start from the ground up." And Napa clearly has great, varied ground.

Ironically, despite Napa's reputation as a Cabernet-growing region, Kathryn didn't relish the idea of living there. The Valley had always seemed snobby to her when she drove down from Mendocino, and that was a turnoff. But she thought then—and knows now—that Napa is the greatest place in the world to grow top-notch Cabernet Sauvignon. So we set our sights on establishing a second residence, this one with a vineyard, in Napa. Thus began our shared journey into the world of wine, and with it, the growth of a shared passion.

Kathryn understood enough about grape growing to know more or less what we should look for in a vineyard. Although we have since learned that there are many wonderful vineyards on the Valley floor that make lush, velvety wines, in those days she thought that a hillside vineyard would produce the most interesting grapes. The theory was that grapes grown in rocky, hillside soil would have to struggle for survival, producing highly concentrated fruit that could be turned into wine with incredible depth of flavor and complexity.

So we set about looking for a vineyard up in the hills.

In 1994, two years after we had started our search, we came across a remote property high on Spring Mountain, with great vineyard land as well as a grapefruit orchard. So we made an offer. When negotiations got serious, we met with the sellers. The family, one of the first partners in one of the Valley's oldest wineries, agreed to the price we offered. The moment the deal was struck, however, the head of the family became very emotional.

"I was born there. I was raised there. Generations of my family have worked that land," he said, the tears in his eyes clearly visible. "I can't imagine no longer having it in the family."

Wow, this is not going to work, we realized. We both understood that with all that emotion, the family was very unlikely to go through with the sale.

Sure enough, the sellers backed out. We were crushed. We had our minds and our hearts set on moving to Napa. Indeed, having gotten so close, we had already envisioned ourselves living on and working that beautiful piece of land. Just as importantly, not having a vineyard had blown a hole in Kathryn's life. On the other hand, we understood. We had gone through that same set of emotions when Kathryn's brother had taken over her family's vineyard.

As the saying goes, "when one door closes, another opens." Eventually our quest brought us to Sacrashe (pronounced "SACK-ra-shay"), a property recommended to us by vineyard broker Paul Spitler. "There's this property you've got to come see," he told us. "It's got a pretty nice vineyard but not a very nice house."

An understatement on both counts. The land without the house probably would have sold faster than the land with the house. The owner had suffered the loss of part of her family in a house fire, so she built a cinder block structure and located it as far as possible from any trees or other flammable landscaping.

The site, on the other hand, was as spectacular as it was secluded. It took a full eight minutes to drive the narrow, winding road through dense, 100-year-old pine and oak forests that connected the hilltop property to the busy Silverado Trail. By the time we reached the top, we felt we were in another world.

Coincidentally, every time we had come out to Napa, we had stayed at Auberge du Soleil, which neighbors Sacrashe. We loved the view from Auberge. But Sacrashe's view, looking out over the central part of the Valley from an elevation that was about 200 feet higher, absolutely stunned us. It continues to astound us—as well as all our guests.

"Oh, my God," people say when they come here and look out at the valley below..

We experience that same sentiment every day. "We're so lucky," we say to ourselves and each other every morning as we watch the white fog blanketing the Valley give way to sun and, in the warmer seasons, 25 to 30 balloons rising up over the vineyards.

When it came to Sacrashe, it was love at first sight. Luckily, the vineyard also had everything we had hoped for: Its high elevation meant cooler days and warmer nights, which would add complexity to the flavors of the grapes. The soil was largely shallow volcanic ash (*tuff*), which meant the roots had to struggle to find water and nutrients, increasing flavor intensity. We didn't yet know how silky and rich the wine from these grapes could taste, but we knew the vineyard was special. It just felt right.

As soon as the sale had been finalized, we started thinking about the house we would build and how we would develop the property. Since art is such a central part of our lives, before we did anything else we identified where we would place various sculptures we already owned and where future acquisitions would best mesh with the topography while highlighting the view. We also spent a lot of time visualizing the infinity-edge pool we wanted, getting down on our hands and knees to see how the land was contoured. We tried to envision how we would design our house and fretted about which architect could give us a clean, modern home that would bring the outside in and still allow us space for the art we loved.

"Look, it doesn't matter," our friend Tom Lardner finally said one evening as we sat outside on folding chairs drinking Cabernet Sauvignon and admiring the valley below. "You can't screw this up."

Luckily for us, since the existing house on the property, athough unattractive, was actually comfortable, our family was able to take up residence immediately. Lupe and Francisco Vasquez, who had worked for the prior owners and who lived with their year-old baby, Daisy, in the caretaker's house, stayed on to become our housekeeper and grounds-keeper. Twenty years later, they are still with us, and feel like family. Daisy, now married with a son and daughter of her own, occupies an office at our St. Helena winery where she arranges tours for guests.

Even though we knew our digs were temporary, we managed to settle into this new place. During the property search, we had been visitors rather than locals. Even once we bought Sacrashe, we still didn't feel like residents. But then we began to figure out where to buy our groceries, take our dry cleaning, and get gas. We learned about St. Helena's farmers' market, which is really cool. And little by little, we began to feel like a part of the Valley.

CHAPTER 3

Jumping In

Now that we had a part-time California home base (then as now we commuted back and forth to Texas), we could focus on making wine and growing grapes.

We had purchased a great vineyard. Before Sacrashe came into our lives in 1995, the property had produced Cabernet Sauvignon grapes for Silver Oak and Cakebread; and Duckhorn—which made one of Napa's most celebrated Merlots—had purchased some of the vineyard's Merlot as well. But was Sacrashe producing the very best grapes it could, or should we try to do something different?

At the outset, we decided to make some wine from our grapes to see what we had. Given that we were without a winery, we opted to begin our wine production with what's called a *custom crush*: a process wherein growers like us effectively rent space from a winery, bringing in grapes and working with the resident winemaker. This is a common practice. We discovered that among the Valley's hundreds of wine brands, only about 250 actually crushed their own grapes. After some searching we learned that Koerner Rombauer, founder and overseer of Rombauer Vineyards, offered custom crush services. Since his reputation in the Valley was impeccable, we called the winery, made an appointment, and went over.

We drove to Rombauer Vineyards, passing by the vineyard planted in front, then climbed up a lovely road off Silverado Trail that winds back and forth up the hill past mature verdant trees before arriving at a rather small parking lot. We parked on the gravel, got out, and walked along a little path that led into the tasting room, where in addition to a mural featuring grapevines at the far end, the walls were adorned with two vintage copies of *The Joy of Cooking,* written by Koerner's great aunt Irma Rombauer, along with memorabilia related to his early flying career.

"We have an appointment to see Koerner," we told the person who greeted us.

Koerner came right out. As one of the most famous people in the Valley, we already knew that his persona is as large as his physical presence. We would find out that he lives large as well. The man knows how to have a good time, a point he made plain that first day.

"Let's go on down and taste some wines," he said by way of greeting.

Koerner, who used to be a pilot for Braniff (an airline we loved) before buying some land and working his way up the hard way, walked us through the winery into the barrel cellar. He grabbed what's called a *wine thief*, a gizmo that allows you to draw wine from a hole at the top of a barrel. He stuck the glass tube, which is about a foot-and-a-half long, into the barrel to fill it up. Holding the top to retain the suction, he poured a sample from barrel after barrel into each of our glasses. Then he commented on the wine we had just tasted before walking us over to the next barrel.

In between wine tasting and wine commentary, we asked Koerner questions about the wine trade, about the industry, and about how he'd gotten started.

"I went into the wine business because it's the only business where you can legitimately drink on the job," he said with a laugh and that irrepressible twinkle in his eye. We've since heard him repeat that line many times.

We quickly figured out that Koerner is honest, that he is fun, and that he has an irreverence about him. He is full of life and embraces it. We love those qualities. *He is just a good guy*, we realized. *We trust him. We like him. This is the right place for us.* Although we already knew of Koerner's stellar reputation and years of experience, we made our decision based on how we related to the man and the fact that his team also seemed great. On the basis of that meeting, our first wine vintages—from 1995 to 2001—were made by Koerner and his team.

Since the process of making Cabernet Sauvignon takes three years from vineyard to sales—the juice must be fermented, aged, bottled, and then left to sit—we wouldn't have our own vintage to sell until 1999. By then we had made a detour—to Vienna.

CHAPTER 4

A Detour

Our surprising turn of events was triggered by a phone call on April 11, 1997, Craig's birthday, from the White House personnel office. We were sitting at the vineyard, enjoying the warm sun and a glass of wine as we discussed changes we wanted to make in the vineyard, when we heard the phone ring.

Kathryn's assistant came outside. "The White House is on the phone," she said.

Kathryn got on the phone.

"How are you doing?" asked Whitney Staley, an engaging 25-year-old woman Kathryn had met a few months earlier at the White House.

"Oh, it is the most gorgeous day here," Kathryn replied. "It's Craig's birthday, it's sunny, and we're having a great time sitting outside."

"Well, your day's going to get better," Whitney said. "Are you available to take a call in about four hours?"

Kathryn affirmed that yes, she would be available then.

"Good. Please be ready."

We knew what the call had to be about. Some eight months earlier Kathryn had begun talking to people in

Washington—especially our close friend, then–Senate leader Tom Daschle—about the possibility of being appointed to an ambassador position. She had lived overseas, spoke other languages, enjoyed foreign affairs, and we thought it would be an opportunity of a lifetime for our family as well as a chance to make a difference through public service.

An ambassadorship isn't something you apply for. You seek out people who are involved in the administration and let them know that you would be interested. Then you try to push that effort along any way you can. That's not easy since the selection process is so obscure. While many ambassadors have been active fundraisers or political donors, there are many more people who have given or raised a lot of money whose wishes to become ambassadors never materialize. In truth, it's a very black box. Nobody knows exactly how each president selects ambassadors, but roughly about a third of the appointments for ambassadorships are non–State Department employees and the rest are promotions from within career diplomatic ranks.

Even though we figured that the White House wasn't calling to turn Kathryn down, this phone call would be the moment of truth. We could think of nothing else in those next hours. Where would they offer? Kathryn had asked for Austria, but you never know.

The phone rang again about four hours later.

"Would you like to be ambassador to Austria?" Marsha Scott, assistant to the president, asked Kathryn.

"I would be deeply honored," she replied.

Instructions followed—including the fact that Kathryn would not be allowed to set foot in Austria before she actually arrived there as ambassador—along with a caveat.

"You are not authorized to tell anybody," Marsha warned.

"You can tell Craig, but you cannot tell anyone else, including your children."

Kathryn hung up the phone. Neither of us could stop grinning.

By the next day, we had started madly researching everything to do with Austria. Today you would immediately turn to Google, but in 1997 that wasn't an option. So we tried to get our hands on every book, every newspaper story, and every magazine article that had anything to do with Austria. Although we couldn't say a word about the appointment, we found ourselves integrating *Austria* into conversation after conversation. Someone would be talking about chocolate and we'd pipe up with the fact that Austrians mix a lot of chocolate into their coffee. Our upcoming tenure in Vienna was so exciting we couldn't contain ourselves.

The White House wouldn't announce Kathryn's appointment until the fall, which meant we had to prepare the kids for our move without telling them why.

"German is just a very good language and you need to know it," we told them when the German teacher showed up at the house. Luckily, they just took us at our word and participated in the language tutoring, no questions asked.

We also had a professor from Southern Methodist University in Dallas come over and give the whole family Austrian history lessons. And we engaged a young woman to teach us how to dance the Viennese waltz. We couldn't tell anybody why we were doing any of this, but we sure had a lot of fun with our clandestine maneuvers.

When it was finally time to leave for our post, we had to drag the kids kicking and screaming. They absolutely did not want to leave their friends. Four years later, we had to drag them kicking and screaming back to the U.S. They absolutely did not want to leave their new friends.

KATHRYN

Certain parts of our lives—like our wine business— had to be put on hold while we were away. We knew we would be setting up a home in Napa and changing our main residence in Texas. We put our Dallas house up for sale and moved some of the furniture to Vienna. We also took much of our art by American artists, to help us share American culture. When I filled out the form specifying where the State Department should return the personal belongings being sent to Austria, I listed our new Rutherford, California, address. Then I cried. It was a joyful and bittersweet moment I will never forget.

Some 20 years later, the thought of that moment still makes me cry. It was big. It was really big. I had moved from California to Texas at the end of the 1970s and had many incredibly wonderful things happen to me while living there, but my heart had also remained in California. Even though I had come out once a month during all that time, I had missed our family's vineyard. Signing that document felt good. Although we would still maintain our principal residence in Texas, where we had our businesses and friends, in four years I would be going home (at least for part of the year) to where I was born and grew up.

We landed at the Vienna airport a few days before Thanksgiving 1997.

"We're stopping on the runway so that the next U.S. ambassador and family can get off here," the captain announced over the plane intercom.

While the rest of the passengers remained seated, we deplaned on the tarmac and climbed into the U.S. Embassy car, driven by Horst Kainz who would be Kathryn's driver and close confidant for four years. Flashing lights and cameras greeted us as we got out of the car at the terminal, and then again in the VIP reception area as Kathryn surprised the attendant press by giving her speech in German.

In many countries the American ambassador is the first among equals in the diplomatic corps and generally one of the more recognized public figures. As a result, that night Kathryn and the rest of us, including our dog Reagan (the only Republican in the family), were on the news everywhere in Austria. And on the front page of the paper the next day and on a regular basis for the next four years.

An ambassador works to deliver and support our diplomatic messages, lead and manage the various departments represented in the embassy (from Commerce to Consulate to Security and more), initiate dialogues on issues of importance to the U.S., support our overseas business interests, and share our culture. Embassies, and in particular American embassies, have a unique opportunity to bring people together and address issues. To that end, within months of our arrival Kathryn held an official breakfast for American author, Holocaust survivor, and icon of the human conscience Elie Wiesel. This was his first visit to Austria since World War II and leaders of the Austrian government attended the breakfast. During the following four years, the embassy led, hosted, and engaged in countless other fruitful discussions on policy matters of import to the U.S.

An ambassador's role also includes showcasing American artists. We held book readings for famous U.S. authors and poets, including Toni Morrison. We sponsored exhibits of prominent U.S. sculptors and painters—including Richard Serra, Jim Dine, and Joel Shapiro—at local museums. We promoted concerts of well-known U.S. musicians such as Wynton Marsalis and hosted the great Walter Cronkite and his wife, Betsy, after each New Year's concert.

The embassy also supported American business, from defense, to pharma, to tourism, to—yes—wine. Promoting California wine is a challenge in Austria, where Austrian wines are oh-so-much better than their German counterparts, French is the standard, Italian is a decent substitute, and South African is what you opt for to be economical. Napa Valley was not on the radar. But the name Robert Mondavi was.

When we heard the Mondavis were coming to Austria, Kathryn invited them, along with business leaders and government representatives, to a dinner at the ambassador's residence. We had not met Bob and Margrit Mondavi before and the chance to entertain the king and queen of Napa was very exciting. The guests assembled. We started the evening with a great Austrian *Sekt* (sparkling wine) and waited for the honorees. And waited. Austrians are very prompt, generally arriving 15 minutes before a party begins. We were pouring more Sekt than our guests wanted and the tension was rising.

All that irritation disappeared almost the moment our honorees walked in, especially once they explained why they were late. The Swarovski crystal company had flown Bob and Margrit from Vienna to another area of Austria earlier that day to talk to them about vineyards, among other things, and the couple had been delayed. Within minutes the group was enchanted. First with Bob, whose presence took over the room as he walked among the guests. Bob was a bigger-than-life guy with a personality to match. He was strong, as well as a little loud, but in a humble kind of a way and it showed. Margrit, who is Swiss born, is elegantly international and has this great laugh. When she speaks English she still has her Schweizerdeutsch accent. At the party, however, she spoke to everyone in her native German, which they loved.

That evening was the start of a wonderful friendship which continued to grow when we returned to Napa. Over the years, Margrit and Bob watched over us and helped us. Little did we know then how much—and how soon—we would need that assistance, a fact which became obvious at another official dinner just a few months later.

CRAIG

Kathy sat at one end of the long table that sat 18 of us, with me, "the trailing spouse" or "just Craig" as I used to introduce myself, at the other.

The ambassador's residence's butler, Christoph, suddenly appeared at my side and leaned in close. "Mr. Hall, you and the ambassador have an emergency phone call from the United States," he whispered in my ear. "I think you'd better take it."

I went into the nearby library and picked up the phone in private.

"You've got to be kidding me!" I exclaimed. I couldn't believe what I was hearing. The Rombauer warehouse, where we were storing all the wine from our small, fledgling wine business—about 1,000 cases of the 1996 vintage and 1,200 cases of the 1997—had caught fire. The entire warehouse, along with our entire wine business, had literally gone up in smoke.

I waited until all the guests had left that night before telling Kathy that our dream of getting more serious about the wine business when we got back from Austria had now been dealt a severe setback. Two years' worth of wine (in fact very good wine) had been totally destroyed. Turns out we didn't have insurance on a loss that totaled $2 million, a misstep we certainly wouldn't make again. But that was just the beginning of our problems. The loss of these two great vintages had jeopardized our ever getting established in the wine business. Could we gain the solid footing we sought after having nothing new to sell for a full two years? We had no idea. We were devastated.

During our tenure in Austria, we held many more such official dinners, though perhaps (and thankfully) few as memorable. We also held a number of events at the residence that were just intended to be fun. While they were not representational, they probably had some diplomatic value. But our intention was nothing more than to create opportunities for people to spend time together. One of these was the continuation of an annual party Kathryn has given for her women friends for almost 25 years.

KATHRYN

We moved to Austria during the holidays of 1997, so I didn't manage to throw my holiday party that year. But the following year I did. Many of my friends in Dallas flew over to Vienna for the party in 1998 and in subsequent years, and the size of the party grew substantially over the years because my new Austrian women friends also attended.

The women's movement came later to Austria, so that first year my Austrian guests had a hard time adjusting to the idea.

"A party just for women?" they asked. "Just for women?"

But they came just the same and found that they loved being able to celebrate the holiday season and network with other women. By the time we left in 2001, the wife of the president of Austria was hosting a women's holiday party of her own.

One of my favorite memories involves bringing in a psychic as entertainment. My close friend Debra Ritchey is a psychic, so she comes and reads at all my parties, including those I threw in Vienna. But I also found an Austrian psychic who could read in German for my Austrian guests. When a lot of my American friends wanted to experience the Austrian psychic, I enlisted 15-year-old daughter Jennifer to translate.

Austrian psychics, it turns out, are much more direct in a social setting than American psychics. "Your husband has been cheating on you with a woman who works for him," the Austrian psychic said in German to one of my longtime friends, a woman Jennifer had known all her life. She gave others similarly disturbing readings.

"I can't say that," Jennifer retorted in German at each unsettling revelation.

"*Du muß,*" insisted the psychic, as my American friends watched Jennifer and the psychic argue in German about whether she would relay the "news" to my friends.

Talk about cross-cultural sharing.

As amazing as our four years were, Craig couldn't wait to return to his Dallas-based businesses, and we both couldn't wait to focus on our now shared passion for wine.

Well, as it turns out, three of us actually returned from Vienna to the wine world. Whitney Staley, who while at the White House personnel office had delivered the news to Kathryn that the White House was going to give her *the* call, had also come to Vienna and worked closely with Kathryn in the embassy. During her time at post she met her now-husband, Jody Jacobson. After marrying in their hometown of Chicago (how coincidental is that?), they moved to San Francisco and Whitney, a treasured part of our lives, became vice president of the winery.

As for Kathryn, after four years of sporadic visits to Vienna's local vineyards where the dirt around the vines had that same musty, dusty smell she had grown up with and loved so much, our return to the vines in Napa signified that she was truly home.

CHAPTER 5

Your Friends Can Only Buy So Much

Upon our return to the States in 2001, we immediately jumped back into our wine venture. Despite losing our 1996 and 1997 vintages we were ready for business, already making pretty good wine, and about to make a lot more of it. We just had to learn how to sell it.

Starting out, we had hired Doug Hill, a viticulture veteran, to manage the vineyard and Rombauer to make the wine. All our other plans for our life and business in Napa had been on hold because we were in Austria. We hadn't even seriously thought about how we would sell the wine we made.

Looking back, that was startlingly naive. Like so many other small producers new to the wine business, we thought we could sell a few thousand cases just to our friends. That lasted about six months. Then our friends stopped buying. Whether you're making 1,000 cases or 3,000 cases, that's a lot of wine. Nobody we know has friends who drink that much.

★ ★ ★

In May 2003, after we had decided to purchase the former Napa Valley Co-op, Craig—the consummate entrepreneur—drafted a business plan and strategy for the winery. He freely admits that his frequent handwritten notes or dictated memos, which sometimes go on for 10 or 15 pages and which he sends to everyone who's remotely involved, drive people around him nuts. This one delineated his vision for our wine business, which included having two Cabernets and a Merlot.

CRAIG

Looking back, I note that my 20-year plan from 2003 projected total wine sales of 370,000 cases. I envisioned having the largest high-end wine club in the history of the world, based on the high quality of wines we would produce. "Our onsite sales are soon to be 20,000 to 25,000 cases per year, with wine club sales being 85,000 cases per year at stabilization," I wrote. "The wine club sales numbers in that range are unprecedented in the industry today, but I still believe with carefully thought-out clubs and the ability to gather relationships, this is a realistic 20-year goal."

Realistic or not, at the time this was a serious stretch. To say that we hadn't sold much wine up to that point would be an understatement. We knew we had to have goals in order to know where we were headed. Still, we had no clue how to sell wine. We just did whatever to try to get a sale here or there. We tried to sell to every friend we had in the U.S. Then we reached out overseas. We had made many friends during the time that Kathryn was the ambassador, so we were able to export some wine to Austria. When we did get an order, we tracked it all on Excel spreadsheets and rang up the orders manually.

We knew so little about the business of selling wine that at the beginning, in 2002, we actually hired someone for the job who had also never worked in the industry. Our assumption was that a good salesperson can sell anything; that idea has some merit, but with a distribution system as complex as the one for wine, you've simply got to know the ropes.

Unlike most consumer products, alcohol is regulated separately by each of the 50 states, with oversight provided by the federal government. The repeal of Prohibition in 1933, which had criminalized the sale, production, importation, and transportation of alcohol, gave each of the states the power in most cases to determine the legal parameters related to alcohol. It's been an evolving process since then. For a winery selling in all 50 states, as we intended to do, that meant we had to deal with a huge, complicated, and ever-changing web of very different laws in different states.

In most states there are three tiers within the industry—the winery that makes the wine, the distributor that has a sales team to call on accounts and sell the wine, and the third tier of *off-premise* or *on-premise* outlets. Wine stores, grocery stores, retail stores, and the like constitute the off-premise tier. On-premise outlets are the restaurants and bars where the wine is sold and consumed. The rules regarding how these tiers can interact differ from state to state. In some states, for example, a winery cannot sell directly to the third tier. Which means that we can't approach stores or restaurants without going through a distributor.

California, the largest market for wine in America, is an exception. California allows you to sell direct. Texas, on the other hand, for years had a whole separate committee of its House of Representatives to deal exclusively with alcoholic beverages. Unsurprisingly, the sale of alcohol in Texas is highly regulated.

Clearly we had a lot to learn.

We didn't even know how to begin to find a distributor. Years before, Kathryn had worked with a distributor to sell wine in Texas that she had made from her family's vineyard. Out of friendship or pity, two of her best friends, Barbara Cottrell and Lee Schepps, who owned the Julius Schepps Company—a revered, very high-quality beer, liquor, and wine distributor in Texas—took her on as a supplier. But locating a California distributor for our winery would prove more challenging. To assist our new-to-the-industry salesperson, we hired someone who had worked as a broker and was in between jobs to advise us. In essence, using a broker adds a *fourth* tier to the three-tier system. Brokers don't ever take possession of the wine but they take a cut of the profit.

Eventually, we began to learn how the industry works.

"Here in California, you can go right into a restaurant," our new consultant told us.

"How much do we charge?" we asked. We had no idea and, up until then, had no way of finding out. There was no reference book to check and we hadn't yet discovered Wikipedia, which had just been launched. We didn't understand standard markups or the importance of looking at a competitive set. We didn't even know who bought the wine in a restaurant. Our consultant explained that most nice restaurants have a sommelier who does the wine buying. But not always. He suggested that Kathryn call up the restaurant and simply ask, "Who buys your wine?" Sometimes it would be the guy that owned the restaurant. Sometimes it was the sommelier. Nice piece of information to have.

By the end of 2001 we had a general idea of what to do, so we started out selling direct in California. It was a tough slog. At the time our fans were few and we had certainly not even hit the radar of the wine critics.

"You have no scores, no reputation, no one has heard of you," the sommelier of a fancy, well-known restaurant told Kathryn early on. "Your wine is good, but so are lots of others. Why should I carry your wine?"

He had a point.

Kathryn started calling everyone she knew in the Bay Area. "Do you know anybody who owns a restaurant?" she asked. "Do you know anybody who works in a restaurant?"

It was like applying for a job, only she was trying to sell a product rather than herself. When she got a lead, she'd load up bottles in the back of the car and drive down to San Francisco where she'd go into the restaurant and try to place our wine.

KATHRYN

I called anyone I knew through any connection who might possibly be able to help or who might know anyone else who could. I even enlisted the husband of my college sorority sister Jan Ritzau, one of my closest friends. I had heard that he was acquainted with some folks who had invested in restaurants in San Francisco. He agreed to spend an afternoon with me, going from restaurant to restaurant and having a glass of wine here and there. Each time we'd ask for the restaurant's wine buyer to come over and, after a quick chat, I'd do the wine pitch. Then my companion would say, "This is really good wine and I'd really appreciate it if you guys would consider carrying it." Sometimes we'd make the sale, sometimes not. Either way, it gave me an early sense of just how personal this business is.

Of course, I was thrilled any time somebody wanted to buy our wine. But trying again and again to place our vintages with little to no knowledge about the industry felt like pushing a string.

When we ran out of people we knew, we started making cold call after cold call. Nobody had ever heard of us. That began to change when Diane Cline joined us in 2003 as our national sales manager. Diane had knowledge, as well as relationships across the country, that helped us significantly.

Diane also expanded our knowledge about the distributor piece of the business, but that didn't help right away. We had so far to go. The distributors were busy and not interested in talking to us. We were too small. We faced the same problem that confronts most small producers. How do you make that breakthrough? Unless you're somebody, they don't want you. But how do you get to be somebody without a distributor?

In 2005, a California distributor agreed to sell some of our 2002 vintage. We had a foot in the door, but over the next two years we didn't get much beyond that. Again, Kathryn turned to her good friend, Lee Schepps, who had helped her years before in Texas (and who now serves on the HALL/ WALT advisory board). When Lee sold his Texas-based company, the head of the premium wine program, a guy named Dennis Barnett, moved to California and became president of the Southwest region for Young's Market Company, one of the nation's largest distributors.

Kathryn called Lee and asked if he might help. Lee called Dennis, and Dennis said, "Have her come talk to me."

Dennis was a godsend. He let it be known throughout the fine wine offices of Young's Market that HALL was a brand he personally wanted to help. Now that we have grown we matter more to Young's Market, but back then we didn't even begin to move the needle. So the sales rep calling on a restaurant and selling wine had no real profit motive to go out and sell HALL. But he was motivated because the boss of his boss's boss said, "This is a priority for me."

That's just how personal it was. Dennis Barnett let the word be known that our brand was important to him and he wanted to move it. And it happened.

Even though we were still in the traditional mode of reliance on restaurants, which boosted both sales and visibility, we had started to open our eyes. And it was fun. Especially since we really liked the wine we had started to produce and sell.

CHAPTER 6

Dreams and Plans for a Small Family Winery

We had dreamed of making wine, which we were now doing. We were even managing to sell it. Still, we hadn't seriously envisioned having a winery until just before our return from Austria. Wow, did we switch gears. In hindsight, we're thrilled we did, but we certainly had no idea of the political travail, business ordeals, and emotional drain in store.

The loss of our wines in the fire had set us back in terms of finances, time, effort, and energy. As a result, our whole winery project had become pretty iffy. But we were not deterred. We had decided that we wanted our own winery in order to control the harvest and production. We planned to locate it next to our home in Rutherford on the east side of the Valley near the Auberge du Soleil hotel. This would turn out to be a massive, time-intensive undertaking. It took more than a year of hard work to get the proper permits. Then it took another year and a half to build a winery and hire the right team.

★   ★   ★

One of our earliest tasks was finding consultants who could lead us in the right direction. Dirk Hampson, one of the partners at Far Niente Winery, was a huge initial help in teaching us how to look for excellence in every detail. Early on, Dirk introduced us to the supportive spirit among vintners in Napa. He continually refused payment, saying he just wanted to help us.

On Dirk's recommendation, we brought in winemaker Ashley Heisey, also a Far Niente veteran, to consult on our winery development. We spent hours talking about winemaking in every aspect. We knew we had a great asset in the vineyard. But how could we make it all that it could be? And how should we develop a winery that was the best we could make it within the constraints we had?

We wanted Ashley to join us as our full-time winemaker, but she was pregnant and not interested in starting a new job. However, she told us she had a friend, Mike Reynolds, who would be perfect. They had graduated from the same class of only 14 people at UC Davis's enology and viticulture school.

Mike had gone on to get an MBA at UC Berkeley while at Schramsberg, where he had worked his way up from cellar rat (the term for someone who labors in the cellar) to general manager and head of operations before turning that role over to Hugh Davies, son of Schramsberg founders Jack and Jamie Davies. Then he had gone to work for Jess Jackson (think Kendall-Jackson and more), who ran what some people in those days dubbed the wine business's "evil empire." (Jess, who was brilliant at creating and marketing brands, was a fierce competitor and a great winery pioneer. In financial terms and in his day, he might well have been the most successful winery owner in the history of the world.)

Mike was a star of the operation as the general manager of Jess Jackson's Stonestreet, a 500,000-case facility, and Vérité, a new Jackson brand that was turning out very-high-end Cabernet Sauvignons. We couldn't imagine that he would be interested in talking to us.

We were wrong.

We met over a glass of wine toward the end of 2002. Mike, at 35 years of age, had a boyish round face and freckles that made him appear even younger. He hardly looked like the person who could be running all those big businesses or who had all that high-level experience behind him. But the instant we sat down with him, we knew that he was a very smart guy who also happened to speak our language. Not only did he seem to have a great value system and great integrity, he was absolutely straightforward. With Mike, what you see is what you get. We all got along great from day one.

CRAIG

I remember when I first met Mike how impressed I was. I had been guessing about—and learning about—a lot of things the hard way, but Mike knew them all off the top of his head. He wasn't the type to brag or to tell you that he knew things. He just knew them.

Kathy and I shared our dreams with Mike, and he shared his with us. The three of us clicked as we had a common vision of doing a high-end, high-quality wine on a very fun basis. He was clearly the guy we wanted to join us.

We told Mike that we wanted to be small and just make 3,000 to 4,000 cases. Maybe we'd go as high as 7,500 someday. That was the plan at the time. Mike liked that because he wanted the challenge of being both the general manager and, going back to his winemaking roots, the winemaker. He missed making wine in his current roles and was tired of working in a big, high-pressure organization. He also thought it would be fun to work with me and learn something about real estate. At least that's what he said then. Today he might regret jumping into the real estate fray with all the fun we've had in some of our deals. I'm being sarcastic here.

Mike officially started full-time with us on November 11, 2002. Our charge to him from the get-go was to find the best wine-related technology and ideas out there. Little did we realize how much his position would be affected by our decision just six months later to buy that big, old winery on Highway 29.

Mike wasn't quite as open in those days as he is now. Today he'd say something like, "That's just the way we roll around here," or "Are you crazy?" Actually, maybe he did say that. I don't remember. I do know that he registered complete bewilderment. (But once again, I'm skipping ahead.)

We had been working on a design for months, but now we could benefit from Mike's expertise. We knew we wanted to create something that was uniquely ours with a connection to our past. But how? Mike quickly shored up our learning curve, which was sorely needed since we didn't even know how much we didn't know.

The winery would be a small facility adjacent to our home and would be located over a cave that we would build. But before we could even break ground, we faced a battle over whether we could build a winery in Rutherford at all. One of our neighbors hired lawyers to stop us from putting in the winery. Extensive legal wrangling ensued. Oddly enough, as soon as we got our final approval, that neighbor put in for his own winery. He's since sold that property to our new neighbor—whom we love. *Karma.*

Next we had to deal with the location of the septic system for the Sacrashe vineyard. Our search for a revised site adequate for septic disposal would end up creating a conflict with a neighboring winery, which was located down the mountain from us. They were concerned that the water from our winery septic system would travel down the hill and end up in their wine caves. Septic systems exist all over the world, and engineers will tell you that the water delivered to a septic system is clean within 3 to 4 feet of its delivery point. This is due to natural filtration through the soils. Unfortunately, the neighboring winery did not agree with that premise. Thankfully, our septic system was ultimately approved and we were again allowed to go forward with the construction of the HALL Rutherford winery.

"Sometimes there are advantages to not knowing because you might be dumb enough to try doing things that otherwise you might never have been able to pull off," Craig often says. That's the long way of saying that ignorance can be bliss, especially in new entrepreneurial ventures. But you don't want to push that too far. So it's always good to find somebody on the team who really knows what he or she is doing, and in those early days that person was clearly all Mike. With his help, we managed to finalize the plans for our Rutherford winery, plans which had originally taken shape in Vienna.

KATHRYN

While I was the ambassador to Austria, I became very close friends with my wonderful driver, Horst Kainz. Over the four years I served there, I probably spent more time with him than anybody else because we were in a car together several hours each day.

One day Horst said to me, "There is a man not far from here who makes the best wine caves in the world. I think you should see them."

Ironically, Horst wasn't so much into wine. He just knew that I was. (In fact the security detail's code name for me was Napa Wine.) So he suggested that we drive down to meet this cave builder.

Friedrich Gruber, whom I'd never heard of, comes from a town outside of Vienna called Gutenstein, which means "good stone." After a 40-minute drive past the beautifully manicured lawns and trees that define the Austrian countryside, we made our way up this long driveway to a lovely stone house that looked very much like a small castle.

Herr Gruber met us out in the front.

"Come in the caves," he said in German.

We descended into his personal cellar, which turned out to be an amazing sort of underground city with cellar room after cellar room. As we went from one to another to another to another, he talked about his craft. He continued talking over lunch during which we shared, *natürlich,* a little wine.

Soon after, Herr Gruber called Horst. "Would the Ambassador ever be interested in having a cave in her California winery?" he asked, since he was already doing other work in the United States.

The Ambassador was interested.

When we met with Herr Gruber in Napa in 2002, we showed him plans for the cave we had envisioned.

"You want there to be drama," the cave maker said. "You need to double the size of the tasting room."

We listened.

Then he said he would bring limestone and bricks over from Austria, which would turn the center tunnel into a unique, beautiful space.

"How much will this cost?" we asked again and again.

"Look, I really want to do this," he replied. "Let's just agree that I won't make money and I won't lose money. It'll be nice and everybody will be happy with everybody afterward."

CHAPTER 7

Building HALL Rutherford

For a brief moment after buying St. Helena, we had actually wondered whether it made sense to go ahead and build HALL Rutherford since we would be making the same wines in both places. In the end, we decided to go ahead.

By 2004, we were finally building the caves and winery at Rutherford. After a couple of years of headaches getting approvals, it was fun to move forward with construction. We wanted the modern, Rutherford cellar tanks, also known as *fermenters,* to contrast with the historical Austrian bricks going inside the tunnel. We also wanted them to be as beautiful as they were functional. We knew that for efficiency and quality reasons, a tank should be almost full when making wine, so we designed the tank sizes to correspond to the sizes of our vineyard blocks.

"Why do tanks have to be round?" Craig asked Mike when we started to think about what those would look like.

"They don't," Mike replied.

Coupling the different size requirements with our space

constraints, since we had to keep the winery building within a 5,000-square-foot limit due to the fire code, led us to trapezoidal tanks that fit into a semi-circle.

The uniqueness of the tanks at HALL Rutherford winery extends past their contemporary shape. The control of temperature during fermentation is one of the most effective tools a winemaker has to produce exceptional wines. Many tanks, to save money, have a heating or cooling belt that covers only the middle of the tank. However you don't have as much control over the process that way. As a result, the grapes at the top of the tank may not be as cool as those in the middle of the tank. In contrast, our tanks have heating and cooling jackets that extend the full height of the tank, allowing for consistent temperature control throughout the tank, along with state-of-the-art controls.

While we were working on the final designs of the tanks, we were also in the midst of building our caves, which lie between the winery's winemaking operation and its tasting room. In the late 1800s, Chinese laborers carved wine caves out of Napa's volcanic rock using only picks and shovels. These days a wine cave drilling machine that looks like a monster Roto-Rooter bores into the hill, breaks up the stone, and pushes the rubble back out on a conveyor belt. Even with that kind of mechanized help, digging out our 14,000-square-foot cave took 10 months.

Once the drilling machine had completed its task, we reinforced the cave to make it earthquake proof. Then we sprayed gunnite on the cave's frequently used surfaces. The rest of the cave's interior was all finished by hand. Laying the limestone and the bricks, each of which is stamped with the Austrian emblem, would take another six months.

Herr Gruber had sent us the bricks that he had reclaimed from buildings constructed during the over 800-year Hapsburg reign. The huge trucks delivering the bricks, however, couldn't make it up our narrow, winding road. So the containers had to be unloaded in St. Helena, and then ferried up to the winery on smaller trucks.

We were excited about the arrival of these historic, handmade bricks that would create our cellar. Mike met the first container as it arrived in St. Helena with great anticipation. He opened it only to discover a large batch of muesli, apparently sent by Herr Gruber to ensure that we would not forget where the bricks had come from. Herr Gruber need not have worried.

Over the next few months, we watched the bricks so reminiscent of our Vienna stay being placed ever-so-carefully throughout the cave with amazing craftsmanship. The arches at cross paths in the winery meet at just the perfect angle. These bricks undoubtedly could have told many stories from their former lives, but we're sure they now feel very welcome and comfortable due to the loving care and respect with which each was placed. They are history and you feel it every time you visit the cave.

The cave turned out better than we could have imagined. Along the pathway from its entrance to the hospitality room, you pass numerous niches. These were empty for the first year; only recently have they all been filled with art. This space is special and we did not want to add art or sculpture that didn't have meaning and that didn't tie to the cave itself. We love all the pieces we selected, but the antique jeroboam wine holder—a gift to us from Herr Gruber—really sums up the story of our cave. Can you imagine? This man builds the cave at his cost on a handshake deal, then gives us a gift upon completion. To this day the three of us are still very good friends. We think the world of Herr Gruber, whom we now call Fritz. When he comes to the States, we see him any chance we get.

Herr Gruber had created not only a spectacular brick cave, but an equally stunning tasting room at the back of the cave. All the latter needed was a chandelier. Naturally, this couldn't be just any chandelier. Initially, Kathryn wanted a Chihuly. Although we love his work, we jointly came to the conclusion that there wasn't a personal connection between ourselves and the artist when it came to envisioning the piece. So, we decided to look into other artists who create chandeliers.

Our close friend Virginia Shore, who has helped us find so much of our art over the years, referred us to Donald Lipski. He had created a big chandelier for New York City's Grand Central Terminal, and Virginia thought we should talk to him. Donald presented us with a drawing of a vine's roots. Dangling from each root were beautiful crystals reflecting light embedded in the root itself. We loved the concept. It was just magical.

The chandelier, which measures 12 feet high and 4½ feet wide, came out so much better than we ever could have imagined. And here is the serendipity of it all. Only once we received the chandelier did we find out that the artist had used Swarovski crystal from Austria. How fitting.

Anchoring our tasting room with that dramatic piece reinforced the notion that having a memorable location where you can establish relationships with guests is the best way to showcase and sell wine. The chandelier became the winery's crown jewel. Of course, we didn't think of it that way at the time. We just thought of the chandelier as one of any number of decisions.

These were fun times. Along with our team, who really came together despite being so young, we were on a mission to finish and open Rutherford. In December 2004 we had a Christmas party at our house for our handful of employees and their families, the youngest of whom was two-month-old Jack, the son of Mike and his wife, Jenny. Those holiday festivities marked the start of an annual tradition.

In early 2005 we were ready to launch HALL Rutherford, and the grand opening celebration assumed its place front and center in our minds. This would be the first time we welcomed the Napa wine community to our winery. In addition, we wanted to make the celebration a tribute to Austria because Vienna had played such an important part in our lives. In many ways, the experience changed us all forever. To be able to bring that home to our winery, where we could be with it all the time, meant the world to us. So during our celebration, we wanted to combine what we loved about Vienna with what we loved about Napa Valley.

For the opening—which the Austrian vice-chancellor, Hubert Gorbach, attended along with Herr Gruber—Ilonka Pusterhofer, who had worked years before at the Ambassador's Residence, offered to come prepare *echte* Austrian food as a gift to us. In a tent we set up behind our house, we sat with our guests and listened to the Vienna Boys' Choir (as luck would have it, they were touring the Western U.S. just then). Our guests also included Austin Hills of Grgich Hills Estate and his Austrian-born wife, Erika, whom we knew from our days in Vienna. After the performance we invited everyone into the cave for dinner and dessert.

Ilonka's food was fabulous. People kept returning for more as they walked through the tunnels. No one enjoyed the food more, however, than the boys in the choir—the *Sängerknaben*. They had looked and sounded like angels during their performance. But when it was over, they became real boys again. They ripped off their robes and ran back and forth through the tunnels in blue jeans, stuffing themselves with Ilonka's good Austrian food. It had been many months since they had tasted *Wienerschnitzel und Kaiserschmarrn*.

At the end of the evening, we sat back exhausted and just looked at each other. We had done it. We had introduced our winery to the world—or at least the world in Napa.

CHAPTER 8

It's All About that Grape

From the start we knew that you need fabulous grapes to make fabulous wine. So after a few years of making wine, we decided that we wanted to upgrade the quality of the fruit from the Sacrashe vineyards.

From working her family's vineyard all those years, Kathryn knew that the flavors and quality of a grape depend on a multitude of factors. Viticulture basics range from sun exposure to water and everything in between. You need to plant so that the sun hits—and ripens—the grapes evenly. Otherwise, at harvest you wind up with ready-to-pick grapes on one side of the vine while the others are still green. You want vines to have the right orientation to the sun, to have just the right amount of shade from the leaves, and for the rows of vines to be just the right distance apart. While our Sacrashe vineyard had proven itself over the years, it needed some upgrading.

Oddly enough, when you're looking to produce fine

wine, you don't want vigorous vineyards that produce tons of fruit. A big yield is great if you're trying to make as much juice as possible for a bulk wine. But as Craig discovered when we walked through the grapevines at Kathryn's family vineyard, the flavors in a grape come from the skin and seed. The higher your skin-to-juice ratio, the more complexity you have to work with in terms of flavors and tannins. So we knew we wanted to produce low yields of small, concentrated fruit. Harvesting less than four to five pounds of grapes off of a vine rather than eight obviously raises the cost of the grapes, but those four to five pounds of grapes are going to be loaded with deep flavor.

Since tighter spacing forces the vines to battle each other for the nutrients in the soil, that's going to correlate to a higher quality berry, just as it does when vines fight for water and nutrients on a rocky hillside. Could we improve *our* grapes if we used the more modern, closer, denser spacing of vines? It was a risk, but we needed to find out. So we ripped out perfectly splendid vines. We had to if we were to up our game and intended to maximize our vineyard.

We could have waited. That would have been the prudent thing to do, especially since replanting meant that we wouldn't have useable grapes for four years. But we wanted to make the best possible wines out of that vineyard as soon as possible.

We would discover that redoing a vineyard like this is part science, part art, and a lot luck.

We needed an expert to ensure that the vineyard we replanted could reach its highest potential. In 2002, we hired viticulturist Phil Freese, Ph.D., who had designed the vineyards for the legendary Opus One. Phil arranged to bring a backhoe out to the vineyard to dig many soil pits so he could look at the structure of the soil, the soil depth, the chemical composition, and the variability within the vineyard site. In addition, we took infrared aerial photography that would help us figure out the *vigor* (growth) patterns of the vineyard, which keys us into how to farm the various sections of the vineyard in order to maximize quality. The satellite overview comes up in red and black—the redder the swirl, the higher vigor potential you have. All this information was then brought together to make recommendations for our upcoming planting.

A vine is often made up of two different types of plant material. The *rootstock* grows below ground and doesn't necessarily produce good grapes, but it is resistant to soil-borne pests and diseases. The aboveground *scion,* the chosen varietal for the planting such as Cabernet Sauvignon or Chardonnay, is more susceptible to those soil-borne pests and diseases when planted on its own. However, graft the scion, which grows tastier fruit, onto the sturdier rootstock and you get the best of both worlds.

You don't, however, want to use just any disease-resistant rootstock. And you don't necessarily want to use a single type of rootstock. A vineyard has a number of different areas that require different plants and different care if it is to produce up to its potential. So each vineyard is divided into blocks— parcels of land with uniform characteristics. Often a vineyard will be planted to a variety of rootstocks due to the variability in the vineyard. So to optimize our vineyard we needed to be certain to match the right rootstock with the different makeup of soil types in the vineyard.

To our amazement, Phil told us that in the 19½-acre area we had decided to replant we had 22 different blocks—some of which were long, narrow, and jagged, others of which were tiny, and still others which looked to be good-sized squares—each with a unique set of growing conditions. His analysis of the blocks determined which exact rootstock would fare the best in each parcel and which Cabernet Sauvignon scion should be grafted onto that particular rootstock. The goal was to make sure that each individual block has the opportunity to make the best wine grapes possible.

To accomplish this, we learned that we had to farm each of the 22 blocks separately in terms of irrigation, nutrients, harvest dates, etc. Grapes just 50 feet apart can require different farming due to the varying growing conditions. Remember that the average size of these blocks is less than one acre, which makes farming inherently inefficient. However, since our goal was to make the best wine possible, we went ahead.

Phil also suggested that we plant the vines in a much tighter configuration than had been planted before. When grape cultivation was introduced to Napa Valley in the mid-1800s, vine rows were planted 12 feet apart to allow horse-drawn equipment to pass through. Over the years that had changed, with most growers planting rows 10 feet apart and dropping in plants every 8 feet. Research revealed that by putting the vines even closer together, you wind up with a better quality grape. So through the 1980s, most Napa Valley vineyards were planted at a row spacing of 8 feet with 6 feet between vines (or 960 vines per acre). More recently, in an effort to grow smaller plants and, in combination with devigorating rootstock, to allow those plants to focus on the production of grape clusters rather than leaves or shoots, vineyard rows were planted even closer together.

A vine is a living creature. It only has so much energy. It can take that energy and spread it among 20 clusters or it can spread among 50 clusters. If all its effort is focused on 20 clusters instead of 50, those 20 clusters are going to have more depth, more complexity, and more flavors.

Phil suggested a planting density of 6 feet between rows and 4 feet between vines, or approximately 1,800 vines per acre. This would clearly increase our costs to plant and to farm, while not measurably increasing our yield since we were deliberately discouraging the production of a lot of big fruit.

After careful consideration, we decided to move forward and planted the vineyard in 2002. Although our planting project was state-of-the-art at its time, we continue to monitor and use technology to make sure that our practices are on the cutting edge, as well as being able to incorporate that technology into the next vineyard that we plant.

Since we want to have access to the best possible fruit for all of our wines, we're continually looking for the very best vineyard properties. If the owner wants to keep ownership of the vineyard, we'll buy the grapes. If the owner is open to selling, we'll consider buying the property. So on a pretty regular basis, we wind up adding to our own vineyard properties. While in recent years a lot of our vineyard purchases have been Pinot Noir and Chardonnay for our

WALT Wines brand, we are constantly looking for any great vineyard opportunity for both HALL and WALT.

Some of the best vineyards are never going to be for sale. Families pass down vineyards from generation to generation. Some of these vineyards are so well respected that the owners or vineyard managers can literally pick and choose whom they sell to. As you will read about later, acquiring a Pinot Noir brand really helped us develop relationships with some of the best growers.

On the Cabernet side, Don Munk—our talented and experienced director of vineyard operations since 2008—has also helped in that department. Not only is he an expert in his field and able to identify great vineyards, he has long-standing ties in the Valley that have helped us gain access to—and relationships with—key properties.

Add to that our gifted director of winemaking, Steve Leveque, and our president, Mike Reynolds—the first a Napa native and the second a longtime Napa resident—and the fact that vineyard owners want their grapes to go into great wines, and you have a winning formula that enables us to acquire grapes from some terrific people and some terrific vineyards. In fact, as we are writing this book, we are now buying from more than 140 different properties.

We don't just buy from these vineyard owners. Don and his team work in tandem with them to ensure that they farm the grapes in the manner that works for the high-end wines we produce.

Having access to the best grapes for our wines is really a critical part of our winemaking. We feel very lucky that we can work so closely with such a wonderful group of properties. We also feel lucky that we can tap into some of the latest and greatest technology, which can be a very helpful tool in the vineyard.

Science is rapidly changing the world of viticulture. We use weather stations to send us information over the Internet about the weather in any given part of our vineyard. If the temperatures are dipping too much in the spring during the critical stages, after bud break for example, we can immediately get frost protection out to the vineyards and save the vines.

During a visit to UC Davis in 2015, we learned that viticulturists are experimenting with a way of watering each root separately, based purely on satellite photos. Today we water by block based on our analysis of the microclimate in that particular section. So our approach is fairly scientific. The fact that you can take a satellite picture and look at the leaves on one vine that's 4 feet away from another vine and decide to treat it differently is just amazing. Once in place, this new irrigation approach—the ultimate in customization—will save water, increase efficiency, and improve the quality of the grapes.

We also understand that the science will only take us so far. One of the sayings in the farming world is, "The best fertilizer is the farmer's shadow." Despite the technological advancements, producing wine remains an art shaped by everyone who touches the grape, from the grower to the winemaker, and dictated by instinct as much as knowledge. To illustrate, after taking all those satellite infrared photographs of the vineyard to measure vine vigor, we shared the findings with Doug Hill, who had overseen the farming on this vineyard for more than a decade before we bought it. "Well, I knew that," he said with a smile and a nod.

As we farm the vineyard today, we focus not only on the health of each block, but on the health of individual vines, as well as that of the shoots and clusters on those vines. We want to make sure that we are not allowing too much fruit to grow on any single shoot, so that every shoot can appropriately ripen each cluster to full maturity. We also tie each shoot to one of the trellis wires so that it's perfectly vertical, until all the shoots are lined up like little soldiers standing at attention rather than growing in their natural crisscross pattern. This process is very labor intensive and very costly, but it allows for the optimum amount of sunlight penetration and airflow. Hopefully, all this translates into great wine.

Oddly enough, instead of watering liberally and providing the soil with tons of nutrients, we also stress each vine so it has to work really hard. That practice funnels even more energy into the clusters of grapes left on the shoots. On the other hand, we don't want to overstress the vine either. So we spend a lot of the growing season managing the stress of the vineyard. Depending on the end goal, at certain times we'll apply more or less stress to the vine.

Since we're after quality rather than quantity, we farm each vineyard to attain perfectly ripened individual clusters. This approach usually restricts yields to three tons per acre or less. To achieve that we not only water less, but once the vines are dormant we'll prune to anywhere between 24 and 30 buds per vine. Those buds that we leave on, which look like rose buds or little bumps on the vine's arms, become the growing points for the shoots (known as *canes* once they harden after a year), which typically hold the clusters of grapes.

But grapevines are more difficult than other crops. You can prune to create two shoots per bud, for example, but invariably three or four or even five shoots might come out. So after bud break in the spring, when the new leaves just begin to grow on the vines that have been dormant, we go back into the vineyard and lop off those extras so that an excess of fruit doesn't compromise the flavor of all the grapes the vine produces that year.

We realize that as much as wine-related science can help us in our quest to produce better and better wine, the tender loving care of the people who work the vineyard and who make the wine will always be critical. Having organic vineyards like ours doesn't implicitly mean that the grapes are better. It does mean, however, that we have to spend more time in the vineyard working on the vines just to make sure they're healthy, and that additional oversight leads to better vineyards and therefore better grapes.

Being in the vineyard all the time allows us to watch it more closely. We can't affect how quickly grapes ripen, for example, but we can manage the quality of that ripening. If the grape clusters are shaded, we know to come back and manipulate the canopy to increase sunlight and airflow by pulling off some of the leaves so more sun can hit the grapes. We're looking for direct sunlight for a short period of time, followed by speckled light that touches the cluster all day long as the sun moves through the sky and the angle of the light changes.

Director of Vineyards Don Monk leads this effort with our winemaking team. Each time our crews pass through the vineyard, we are making an adjustment in the vines. During green drop, for example, which takes place as the grapes are beginning to soften and change color, the vineyard crew will go through the vineyard and *drop*, or cut off, the grape clusters that are still green, leaving behind the clusters with darker berries. This helps even the ripeness of all the clusters in a vineyard by removing the less ripe clusters that may have green flavors or unripe tannins. In some high years, a green drop can comprise as much as 20 to 25 percent of your crop (half to one ton per acre) and all those clusters are simply dropped in the rows between the vines. The first time Craig saw this, he nearly had a heart attack because of all of the lost fruit on the ground and the financial implications of that. Now, he understands that this is simply a step along the way to make great wine.

All the while, we're manipulating stress through irrigation, canopy management, and more. We want the vines to shut down and stop putting energy into growing leaves and canopy, and to transition into using energy to ripen the fruit. At this point we hit what we hope is cruise control. If the weather cooperates, we just stay out in the vineyard to assess its overall health and stress, and eventually to determine when we want to harvest.

That's a big if.

As recently as 10 to 15 years ago in Napa, there was a formula for wine growing that specified when you pruned, when you lopped off the shoots, etc... But vines don't behave

according to a formula. They do what they want to do, especially depending on environmental influences. If it's a dry
year they're going to respond differently than if it's a wet year.
Ditto if it's a hot year, a windy year, or if there's a lot of fog.
So there is no substitute for being out in the vineyard to see
the evolution of things. You can't script how you're going to
farm the vineyard. You have to react.

In our vineyards, beginning with pruning and ending
with harvest, somebody touches the vines at least eight times
every year, as opposed to the more typical four or five passes.
Many operations will go through and do a single canopy
management pass, for example, and call it good. Not us.
Throughout the season we go through the vineyard again
and again.

As the grapes approach maturity, different pieces of equipment help us decide when we're going to harvest various
blocks within a vineyard. However, winemakers at the very
highest end of the wine-quality spectrum who work at the
best vineyards don't pick strictly by analysis or a measurement
from a machine, because that tells them nothing about the
potential quality. If you want to follow a recipe, then you
pick according to the sugar percentage or the titratable acidity
or the pH of a grape. But human taste and human intuition
are the best equipment available when it comes to deciding
when to harvest. So Don and Steve walk through each vineyard and each block before making the call to harvest. They
pick a grape and taste it, testing ripening patterns, flavors,
sweetness, thickness of the skin, maturity of the seed, and,

perhaps most importantly, tannins. Then they move and taste another, then another and another after that.

Rain or shine, we handpick our grapes to be sure that every cluster going into the picking basket is ripe. A perfect cluster of Cabernet Sauvignon is going to have the same dark blue color all the way through. A machine can't yet judge that, just as it can't judge whether the cluster has mold inside it due to untimely rain. By handpicking each cluster, we ensure that each berry arrives at the winery in the best condition possible. According to UC Davis, robots with the ability to discern the fruit's characteristics and uniformity may wind up being able to delicately pick grapes in the near future, carefully cutting them off and depositing them in the picking bin. For now, since that's all still conjecture, we rely on humans to deliver intact, unblemished grapes to our crush pad as quickly as possible.

The most impressive Napa Cabernet Sauvignons have texture, concentration, density, and richness; all of which are derived from tannins—that compound in the grape skins and seeds. Steve and Don focus on the quality, maturation, and ripeness of tannin. Some winemakers try to minimize the amount of tannin in their wine to avoid hardness and astringency (a mouth-puckering dryness in some wines), but Steve believes if you harvest grapes with mature tannins then you can't have too much of a good thing—and we agree. The key is to farm the vineyard to produce grapes with mature tannins in both the skins and the seeds. Which brings us back to vineyard site, rootstock selection, scion, irrigation, crop levels, and attention to detail in farming. Everything matters.

Therein lies so much of the skill of working a vineyard. This is not done by rote, it's done by feel and experience. Technology can help fine-tune that, but at the end of the day, the dedication of the team working with the grapevines impacts the quality of the fruit the most. That's what counts because in the end, it's all about that grape.

CHAPTER 9

Dreaming Big

With the replanting of the Sacrashe vineyard and our Rutherford winery construction moving forward in 2003, our wine dreams were beginning to be realized: The opportunity to make a Cabernet Sauvignon that we hoped might someday be considered among the best in the world; a vineyard we could walk through and smell, taste, touch; a winery that would combine state-of-the-art production and beauty; and caves that reflected one of the most exhilarating periods of our lives—now those are dreams. We were *not* looking for another property where we could make wine. We just wanted to finish Rutherford. But when Craig drove down Highway 29 on his way to lunch on that sunny April day, another dream in the making just jumped right out at him, and wound up enveloping us both.

That night when he went to bed, Craig's mind immediately skipped to the old buildings and the outside tanks. Suddenly, instead of the cracked cement interlaced with weeds, he began to see the details of a rebuilt winery fronted by a vineyard. He envisioned gardens and a modern winemaking facility with tanks inside beautiful buildings.

As we dreamed and discussed Craig's find over the next days and months, we also tried to dig up more about this old facility's history. The more we learned, the more exciting the winery became. Our Rutherford winery would have Austrian history in its bones—well, bricks. But the history of this property on Highway 29 was pure Napa Valley.

In 1910, Theodore Gier, a liquor dealer and German transplant, had purchased the whole winery for just $10 and promptly enlarged its capacity by adding on to existing structures and building new ones. He would wind up going to jail and paying $1,500 in fines for Prohibition violations. After Prohibition and just nine years of ownership, Gier sold the property that would become the Napa Valley Co-op and Napa's largest winery in its day.

The Napa Valley Co-op was conceived in a distinctly humble way when, in August 1933, grape grower Charles Forni refused to accept the low price he had been offered for his grapes. He realized that Prohibition would end as soon as the country's new president, Franklin Delano Roosevelt, whose campaign platform had included repealing Prohibition, took office the following January. Rather than sell his grapes for next to nothing ($7 a ton, an absurdly low price even in those days), he decided to start a cooperative winery to help create a market for all those tons of hard-to-sell California wines and grapes.

Forni and a group of growers leased what had been the Gier winery in 1933, substantially increased its fermentation and storage capacity, and produced 500,000 gallons of wine. In 1934, the property was renamed and began to operate as the Napa Valley Cooperative Winery (Napa Valley Co-op) with 142 members. During its first years of operation, the

Napa Valley Co-op did $900,000 worth of business and crushed some 5,600 tons of grapes. By 1935, the Napa Valley Co-op crushed and marketed about 40 percent of the entire grape production of Napa Valley. Within three years of its founding, the co-op had become the largest wine-making facility in the Napa Valley, enabling countless growers to survive during the hardest years of the Napa Valley wine industry.

After World War II, the co-op, like much of the Napa Valley wine industry, experienced a slowdown in sales resulting in a large inventory of unsold bulk wine. An unannounced visit in 1949 by two Central Valley winemakers, Ernest and Julio Gallo, changed the fortunes of the co-op and the path of Napa Valley agriculture forever. Impressed with the quality of the wine that they tasted while visiting the co-op and in need of substantial quantities of bulk wine to improve their San Joaquin grapes, in 1950 the Gallos entered into a contract with Forni and the co-op to purchase 200,000 gallons of bulk wine. By 1951, the co-op sold the Gallos more than 40 percent of the wine produced at the St. Helena facility. The next year, the Gallo brothers contracted to buy the entire production of red and white wine (700,000 gallons). The co-op processed between 4,000 and 5,000 tons of grapes that same year. Over the years, and until 1994 when it sold the winery to Golden State Vintners (Edgewood Winery), the co-op would operate close to its capacity of 2.8 million gallons, all of which it sold to the Gallo brothers.

If you trace the history further back, in 1885 a sea captain named William Peterson started a winery on that land, which already boasted a vineyard from 1873, but which had fallen into disrepair. He, along with his wife and five children, settled on this property in an area that was then called Vineland. Twelve years later, the Petersons completed the winery and fairly quickly thereafter went broke. (The wine business has never been easy.)

The winery was sold to the second owner, Mr. Bergfeld, a German-born contractor and builder from San Francisco, who chiseled out the Peterson name carved in stone at the winery entrance and replaced it with his own. The carved letters that spell out Bergfeld remain there to this day.

CRAIG

In 2003, Edgewood was owned by Golden State Wine Co., a small public company that didn't have huge trading volume and that also owned a handful of large-capacity wineries. Most were making high-volume, low-quality wine, and were located in central California.

Now. How to get the owners to sell us the winery.

As I sometimes do, I approached the problem in an overly complex manner. Instead of contacting the owners to find out if they might be interested in selling, I thought I would try to buy enough stock so that I became a meaningful shareholder. Then the management of the company would have to listen to my proposal to perhaps trade my stock for this winery.

I knew I could only buy stock if I didn't have any insider knowledge, and besides, I had a plan. So without any further investigation I started immediately buying shares every day. The stock traded in such small amounts, however, that it was very hard to accumulate much volume.

Ten days later, as I was still slowly but surely acquiring stock and frequently stopping by the property I knew that somehow we were going to purchase, I happened to meet with a friend. Vic Motto, co-founder, chairman, and CEO of Global Wine Partners, was one of the most experienced winery and vineyard investment banking brokers in the area. He had advised me on some winery matters in the past, and tried to sell me various properties. That spring day, we had broached a wide variety of topics in his office when Vic suddenly started to laugh.

"I really don't know how I'm going to sell this new property I just received the exclusive listing on," he said. "It's huge, but it's a really tough, ugly property that just doesn't fit into Napa. I have no idea how I'm going to find a buyer for it."

Then he showed me a picture of the former Napa Valley Co-op.

"We're your buyer," I told him.

When Kathryn first drove into the hodgepodge of factory-style buildings, she flashed on Craig's first book, *The Real Estate Turnaround*. The book, which he wrote at age 28, was about taking small buildings and rooming houses and turning them into salable, profitable real estate ventures.

This is a real estate turnaround, she thought to herself. The co-op was all about volume over quality. Everything in the facility was large—huge, in fact. From the giant outdoor tanks to the way grapes were brought in and dumped off of big trucks, this was a place geared to making higher-volume and lower-quality wine. We had a lot of work ahead of us, making our style of wine in this great big winery located on Highway 29 where the big-boy wineries play.

Apart from our appreciation of its stellar location, we didn't have a lot of knowledge about the property at that point. We certainly didn't have a business plan or even a thought about one. We just had a gut instinct. We would figure out a way to make this a high-end wine production facility and at the same time a beautiful property.

A short few days later, we signed the paperwork. Among the many surprises the 33-acre former co-op property would hold for us was the quality of the surrounding 14-acre vineyard and the discovery of the walls and partial second floor of the property's original 1885 winery. We were now proud owners of a ghost winery, the name given to wineries built from 1860 to 1900 during Napa's first wine boom.

Our dream grew bigger daily. We would make top-quality wine in a quantity larger than we could at Rutherford. We would do what we were already planning for Rutherford, but we would do it on steroids. We actually did not need to complete the Rutherford winery as we could have made the wine from the Sacrashe grapes at our St. Helena winery. However, we were emotionally committed to that jewel-to-be that was so much a part of our Austrian experience.

Once the purchase had been finalized, we were like a dog catching a fire engine. Now what? We often joke about how we "lied" to Mike and got him to leave a huge operation so that he could come run a tiny little operation, which is what he wanted. And then less than six months later we were on the road to becoming a pretty good-sized place ourselves. All that calm he wanted never happened.

Over the next couple of months, we immediately started to revamp the existing tasting room. And instead of custom crushing our Sacrashe grapes until Rutherford was finished, we started to make wine in the equipment that was still on the St. Helena premises. We had county permits to make more than a million cases at St. Helena, but instead we made only 2,000 cases. Our handful of barrels looked totally ridiculous in the corner of that vacant monster facility.

Still, we felt like we had really arrived. That didn't mean that we weren't all pitching in and working odd hours. Starting a business from scratch is hard and we now had not one but two wineries that were far from being fully operational. So we all did what we had to. Kathryn, our son, David, and several others on our small team manned the tasting room, while Mike, our winemaker and general manager, did every other task imaginable.

In July, right after we had closed on the property, we remodeled the Edgewood tasting room and reopened a month later with a party for our small team and around 30 friends. Bob and Margrit Mondavi came, which excited our employees to no end.

Each passing day cemented the notion that we would share the wine we made along with the beauty of the Napa setting and the art we love, and use architecture to highlight all three. We just didn't know the details of what that would mean.

"If we're going to do this, the winery has to be a *wow*," Kathryn had told Craig. "It has to be an exciting building. We need to work with a great architect."

Craig was right there.

"You know, if I could have any architect in the world, the one I would like to ask would be Frank Gehry," added Kathryn, whose love of great architecture that integrates the space around it had prompted her to follow architects from the time she was very young. "I think his work is simply thrilling."

It's not necessarily good business to engage the world's most famous architect, so she was only half-serious.

"That could be really interesting," Craig said.

We're going Gehry, we agreed.

Frank arrived in Napa with his #2, Edwin Chan, on an atypically overcast summer day in 2004. We were already at the winery, which, despite being located on the Rodeo Drive of Napa Valley, was deserted. The tasting room was open, but at the time it was hardly a space one wanted to linger in.

We were standing about halfway back on the property when we saw Frank get out of his car, his gray hair as wild as his architectural designs. Dressed in black pants and a black T-shirt, he looked like an artist, but a rather avuncular one. Even though he was in his mid-seventies then, there was an almost childlike twinkle about him. He walked over to us and said a polite hello, but he was clearly more interested in the setting than in us.

Our friend Ray Nasher, one of the greatest collectors of sculpture in the world, once told us that art made him see. We got the same feeling watching Frank. He *saw*.

We chatted a little, but Frank stayed focused on the backdrop of the winery, the beautiful Mayacamas Mountains bordering and defining the western edge of the valley. Suddenly, without a word, he scurried over to one of the old fermentation tank's rickety steel stairways, and scampered up to the top and then down to the end of the catwalk. Craig, not being fond of heights and leery about the structural soundness of the stairway and catwalks, opted to stay on the ground. However Edwin, Kathryn, and three Hall Financial Group colleagues ran right behind Frank and headed up, wanting to see what he was seeing and how he was looking at it.

Upon reaching the top, they realized what had propelled Frank up the tank. Experiencing the Valley from a raised perspective was totally different. On the valley floor you feel the caressing breeze and smell the vines and the dirt. When you are 35 feet high, you sense all that, but you also experience the length and flow of the Valley along with its mountainous borders. Craig took their word for it.

"This is what you want," Frank announced. "You want to see the Valley from up here."

Right then we knew that no matter what the winery's design, when you viewed the Valley from the tasting room, you were going to be two stories high. We couldn't wait to see what Frank would come up with next.

Frank told us that he would start work on some drawings and get back to us. Then we didn't hear from him. And we didn't hear from him. We would call his office, but never get him on the phone. This went on for about a month. Frank Gehry was filling our world, but Frank Gehry was not returning our calls.

"This isn't working," we said to each other.

So with immense regret, considering how in love we were

with Frank, we decided to fire him. We planned out our script.

"This is, for us, much more than a business," Kathryn would tell him. "This is something we love and this is a very big part of our lives. We are very committed to this project. And we have to have a partner who feels as passionately about it as we do. You don't feel it, Frank. So although there is not an architect in the world we admire as much as you, this is not working for us."

Kathryn placed the call. An assistant answered and tried to put her off. It seemed like we wouldn't even be able to get Frank on the phone to dismiss him, but something in Kathryn's tone of voice suddenly compelled his assistant to put Frank on the line.

"Hello, this is Frank Gehry," he said. "How is everything going?"

"Frank, not well."

"Now, you've had some difficulty getting a hold of me? My secretaries are not working out. I've really had problems with secretaries. But I'm looking forward to our working together. I think we're going to have something to show you in one month's time. How does that sound?"

"It sounds pretty good," we said, caving at the first instance of recognition.

Then Frank gave us his personal cell phone number and just like that we were back in love. Several weeks later, we received the first of what would be many drawings.

We loved every design Frank came up with. Some weren't very practical, but they were beautiful. At one point he suggested that the tanks should be made of glass so you could look at the wine as it fermented. That would have been

The HALL Wines
"Bunny Foo Foo," by
Lawrence Argent

Napa Valley Cooperative,
the forgotten child

Sacrashe Vineyard, our
first Napa Valley vineyard,
purchased in 1995

Brijetta, David, Kathryn,
Craig, Independence, and
Jennifer in Vienna

Building the HALL
Rutherford caves

Vineyard president Mike
Reynolds, shortly after joining
HALL in 2003

The HALL Rutherford tank room entrance to the wine cave

Our 16,000-square-
foot Austrian brick
wine cave

The Wiener Sän-
gerknaben (Vienna
Boys' Choir) at the
opening of HALL
Rutherford

Austrian vice chancellor
Hubert Gorbach (left)
with the Halls and Fritz
Gruber under the chan-
delier at the Rutherford
opening

Former chef at the U.S.
Embassy in Vienna, Ilonka
Pusterhofer, and Craig

Cabernet Sauvignon (left) and Pinot Noir (right)

Our son, David, setting the Sacrashe Vineyard drip system

Director of wine-making Steve Leveque and director of vineyards Don Munk doing regular vineyard inspections

The only surviving photo of the original Peterson Bergfeld building

Napa Valley Cooperative, circa 1936

Our first (and not so successful) stab at tasting room uniforms

We did everything we could to attract customers to HALL St. Helena

Senator Tom Daschle and
Robert Redford sharing
political stories at HALL
Rutherford

Craig with daughters Independence
and Jennifer

With daughter Brijetta and
her husband, Parker, at an
annual harvest party

There is
nothing better
than a party
when harvest is
over

The Napa Valley barrel auction hosted at HALL St. Helena in 2015

Napa Valley royalty—Bob and Margrit Mondavi—at a Hall family harvest party

The HALL St. Helena hospitality building today

The approximately one acre of photovoltaic cells atop the HALL St. Helena winery roof

Sculptor Patrick Dougherty directing the installation of "Deck the Halls" at HALL St. Helena

A Cabernet Sauvignon night harvest

Bringing in the grapes

Harvest

Longtime cellar worker Celfo
Guzman and stacks of RFBs
(see Glossary, page 206)

Sauvignon
Blanc grapes at
the beginning
of the sorting
process

A HALL tradition: blessing the first grapes of the harvest

Director of winemaking Steve Leveque hand sorting Sauvignon Blanc grapes

Using the state-of-the-art optical sorter for red grapes

Doing a pump-over

A close-up view of a pump-over

The HALL St. Helena
crush pad during harvest

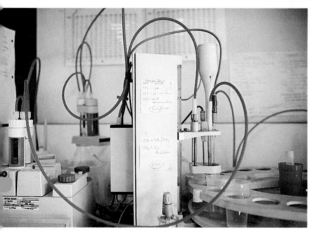

An auto titrator

WALT winemaker
Megan Gunderson Paredes
and director of
winemaking Steve
Leveque blending

Wine analysis

Associate wine-
maker Alison
Frichtl, checking
the wine cap

Our 100-point
production
team at HALL
St. Helena

Using a barrel
thief to sample
wine

Kathryn Hall Cabernet
Sauvignon being bottled

Kathryn Hall
Cabernet
Sauvignon
being labeled

HALL St. Helena tasting room art by Spencer Finch

At HALL St. Helena, "Garden Plot" by Nick Cave

WALT winemaker, Megan, and our daughter Jennifer shooting HALL & WALT news

Our all-star HALL and WALT team

Our first 100-point wine, 2010 HALL Exzellenz Cabernet Sauvignon

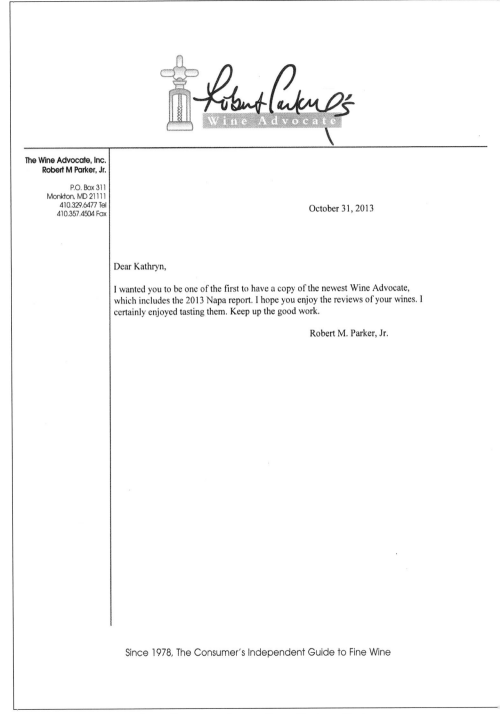

The Wine Advocate, Inc.
Robert M Parker, Jr.

P.O. Box 311
Monkton, MD 21111
410.329.6477 Tel
410.357.4504 Fax

October 31, 2013

Dear Kathryn,

I wanted you to be one of the first to have a copy of the newest Wine Advocate, which includes the 2013 Napa report. I hope you enjoy the reviews of your wines. I certainly enjoyed tasting them. Keep up the good work.

Robert M. Parker, Jr.

Since 1978, The Consumer's Independent Guide to Fine Wine

A perfect score letter, from Robert Parker

stunning, but it was pretty impossible. Winemaking demands tanks that are temperature controlled.

Still, he brought fresh eyes to our project. By 2007, after years of expensive designs, he came up with a drawing featuring a big, crazy basket-weave roof that we loved. We just couldn't find a natural material that worked.

We had promised our neighbors we would not use titanium or other forms of metal, which is what Frank usually uses for the rooftops of his buildings. We wanted to be more indigenous to Napa. Edwin, who had worked with Frank on the Guggenheim Museum in Bilbao, Spain, and who was very involved in our project, thought that we could do a wood trellis that would be bent like metal. Frank expressed his doubts about whether that would work. We spent a huge amount of time, effort, energy, and money putting together these massive wood trellises, which we then hung on steel girders at the back of our property so that they could go through different seasons and weather. They failed the test in every possible way. They cracked, they bent wrong, they got water in them. So the idea never worked, which was a part of the reason we ultimately did not go in that direction.

That wasn't our only problem related to the winery design. It never occurred to us that Frank Gehry would be controversial.

The winery building Frank designed for us would have replaced a sea of rusting, 1950s-era wine storage tanks that had been littering our back vineyard. Yet our neighbors, along with some other locals, preferred the tanks to anything Gehry designed. Clearly the spirit of NIMBY—Not In My Back Yard—was alive and well in Napa Valley. We did get the support of many key people, especially Bob and Margrit

Mondavi, who put their reputation and name behind us. But that didn't silence the protestors.

We continued to hope that once we had figured out a way to build Frank's wonderfully wild winery design, those who opposed it would come around. We also hoped that his design would attract the visitors that were definitely not coming in droves. We had put out our sign after transforming the tasting room and waited for people to start flooding in. They didn't. We learned during that first season that you can have a great location, but without great wine and a brand, no one really cares. Our one sales advantage seemed to be with people who shared our last name, many of whom suggested that they should get a family discount.

CHAPTER 10

More than Just a Wine Factory

There is no substitute for making great wine. It's what's in the bottle that counts. While you can figure out how to attract visitors to your winery or sell just about any wine, the pride comes from making a wine that is truly special.

Part of that attempt to create top-notch wine involves competitive tastings to see how our wines stack up against wines from other wineries. Our winemaking team and some others on our winery staff taste and grade wines from four or five flights—each of which features six to eight samples—taking notes on each. This is where learning to properly spit out one's wine is critical, since drinking all that vino would compromise the process and lead to a whole lot of trouble.

During the tastings, we go around the room so that each person can offer descriptions of the smell, flavor, and taste of each wine. There are no wrong answers, but there are certainly answers that are more educated than others. Kathryn delves into the nuances of exactly how to describe the various flavors in wines. As for Craig, he's just gotten to the point where he can tell if a wine is corked or not. He can tell whether or not to recommend it to someone who wants a dry wine, a sweet wine, a full-bodied wine, or a lighter wine. In short he knows the basics, but he still lacks the sophisticated palate that professional winemakers share. So when it comes to the tastings, he jokes that when all the tasting notes are collected, his are secretly thrown in a wastebasket. In fact, knowing that the votes will be averaged and feeling that his aren't as good as either the winemakers' or Kathryn's, Craig often throws them away himself.

CRAIG

I may not be a pro when it comes to wine tasting, but I know if I like a wine or if I don't. And that's what counts. I always tell people that at the end of the day, the most important thing is whether or not the wine tasted good to them. While it is useful for us at HALL Wines and WALT Wines to hold these high-level, sophisticated tastings, we believe wine is really about personal enjoyment. In that sense, maybe my palate is actually important.

Of course, the tastings that can make or break a wine—or at least its sales—are those conducted by the professionals who share their opinions with the public. Wine critics may seem like gods to vintners like us, but they are only human. Even a wine critic with the best palate can taste a wine one day and have a different reaction the next day, depending on dinner the night before, breakfast that day, and plain old mood. Couple that with the vast array of wonderful wines out there, and great wines will inevitably get overlooked.

So while high scores are wonderful, and while we were certainly striving for our share, we knew we couldn't rely on them for long-term success. We needed to build a brand that people connected with and recognized, one based on wines crafted according to our style.

This wasn't just about the wine. Our name would be on those bottles, so it was personal. It still is. So we needed to create a brand and an experience that reflected who we are.

From the beginning, we would sit around talking about why the world needed another winery and what it would take to make us different, worthy, and relevant. In 2006, we met with Duane Knapp, a branding consultant, to help us define exactly who we were and what HALL Wines stood for.

Our small team consisting of Mike and a few others gathered in the wine room of our house. After quick introductions, Duane took us through a soul-searching exercise to figure out the future of our brand. Great Napa wineries each express their own personalities, and the winery owners, or vintners as they are often called, are a critical part of that personality. Robert Mondavi was the maverick who did things his way. At Frog's Leap, John Williams's sense of humor comes through in everything he does. Quintessa exudes international elegance, just like proprietors Agustin and Valeria Huneeus. The natural, flavorful wines of Chappellet are reflected in their tasting room's personal, family-style vibe, which completely fits Donn and Molly Chappellet and their family. We needed to figure out how to translate our personalities into our brand.

Working with a branding consultant is really like seeing a psychiatrist. Since a solid brand is based on who you are, you have to know yourself in order to develop it. Over the course of several sessions, we mapped out our sense of who we are as people along with our winery-related aspirations. Whenever our team met—whether we were down in our wine cellar or seated around our dining room table—we'd sip our wines and scribble words on sticky notes which we affixed to poster boards.

"Who are you?" Duane asked the eight of us again and again. "Give me words. I just want words. Who are you? Why do you exist?"

Today we have a much easier time answering that question, but back then it wasn't easy to come up with terms that really pinpointed the essence of our winery. Slowly, however, they started to emerge.

We had figured out by that point that we wanted to convert our vineyards to organic farming. Not only was it better for the land, it was better for the health of our workers in the field, who at that point included our son. So *organic* was one of the words. It worked not only because it specified how we farm, but also because our growth was—and has continued to be—organic. As opportunities come our way, we grow. We learn more and we grow some more.

Quality was another word that surfaced immediately, but what did that really mean?

Terms that defined us as people were harder to identify. We knew that we loved the land and truly cared about the quality of wine we produced. We also knew that we felt a personal connection to the process. We knew we weren't stuffy and that we loved being around people. But summing all that up in just a few words was daunting and required serious self-analysis as well as time.

One thing had been clear from the start: We wanted our winery to be more than just a production facility. We wanted it to reflect our passions for nature, art, and architecture.

Craig, the son of an art teacher, had started collecting art as a teenager. Until we met, Kathryn considered art as too extravagant to buy for the home. Rather, it was something she would go to see in a museum. Now we collect art together, and that is perhaps the most time-intensive and fulfilling passion we share outside of work. Without it, life would seem flat and empty. We also love to share the paintings and sculptures we've acquired—in our home, businesses, and public spaces and, yes, in our wineries. At the entrance to our St. Helena HALL Winery, for example, you will see a round wall hanging by artist Nick Cave measuring 17 feet in diameter and made out of bits of bejeweled fabrics. Even though we didn't have a wall big enough for it, we bought this work as an anniversary gift for each other in 2010. It sat in a very big wooden box in the basement for five years, until we built our new winery facility at St. Helena and created a wall that would serve as the perfect backdrop.

Art can go everywhere—in the garden, by the parking spaces, among the grapevines, in the tasting rooms, in our production facilities, and in offices that are only visible to the staff. Hopefully it's enjoyable and stimulating for the people who visit as well as for all of us who work here. So we never questioned whether or not including art at our wineries was a good or bad idea. Art was a critical component from day one. We wanted to share something that is a personal and immensely important part of our lives. Which is exactly how we think about the wine we make and the wine setting we've created.

People have helicoptered to HALL Wines to propose to their beloved. We've hosted countless wine education events that people have turned into anniversary and birthday celebrations. People return for the wine, as well as for the sensory experience of being at the winery itself and the enjoyment of the setting.

We love when we get feedback from our winery guests saying that they feel a connection not just to the wines and their winery experience, but also to the winery team. Participants in the wine tastings and dinners Kathryn holds each year across the country regularly describe to her their winery visit in great detail, right down to the name of the wine educator who hosted them and why he or she was so special.

Wine is more than just a product. It isn't something that people tend to drink like they do Coca-Cola or even a martini. It is so often consumed as a part of a celebration that it frequently creates or involves memories. So the particular taste of a specific wine often becomes tied up with emotion. Countless times we've heard folks exclaim that they're crazy about a particular wine and then go on to describe the associated experience—they met a great love, closed an important deal, or experienced another great milestone in life.

In the end, wine is part product and part happening. That makes it different from any other business we know. It also means that not only are we in the business of growing grapes and producing and selling wine, we're also in the business of taking care of people and creating experiences.

Wine and Napa are about helping people enjoy their lives a little more. So that's part of our job. In 2015 our hospitality team started The Art of the Blend—a regularly scheduled tour where, after tasting a number of different wines to blend from, guests create and bottle their own blend and take it home. They essentially get to play winemaker for a day. Now we don't expect to find a Steve Leveque on these tours, but they're a blast and they help make our wines approachable. Providing that kind of interactive, entertaining wine experience is a key value for us. We never want to be regarded as snobby. It's just wine, after all. It's meant to be fun.

We want to reflect that sense of casual fun with our marketing. In July 2015, for example, we sent out an email campaign slugged *Playing Now: HALL Summer Blockbusters.*

"Pop the popcorn, pour a glass & press play!" read the email. "Summer is in full swing. Kick back and stay cool with the best pairing around: HALL wine and summer movies!"

The rest of the email offered wine pairing suggestions, not for food but for the type of movie you wanted to curl up with. Our 2011 HALL Darwin Red Wine was suggested for action movies: "Just like a nonstop action film, this wine will keep you on the edge of your seat. Darwin embodies the dark, muscular, earthy interpretation of Syrah." Romantic comedies were paired with our 2013 HALL T Bar T Ranch Sauvignon Blanc: "Playfully bright with layers of tropical and stone fruit. Our T Bar T Ranch Sauvignon Blanc is a surefire way to add freshness and energy to your favorite romantic comedy!"

We want our team to have a fun approach to wine. People work in this industry for financial reward, of course, but they also work out of passion. Most everyone here could be making more money elsewhere. Hopefully they share with our visitors the love of wine that brought them to Napa and help all involved to have a darn good time while they're at it. That's certainly our goal, despite having been severely tested on more than just one occasion.

CHAPTER 11

Negotiating Napa

When we purchased our St. Helena winery, we couldn't wait to improve the ramshackle property. Even though we had struggled with a handful of long-fought objections from our neighbors at the Rutherford winery, we didn't anticipate problems at St. Helena. We simply figured that the St. Helena winery neighbors, to say nothing of the county, would be just as excited as we were to see the historical aspects of the facility restored and all those nasty tanks replaced with something beautiful. To our surprise, we soon realized that many people whose homes bordered the winery were decidedly displeased.

So we pulled back and reached out to neighbors and the community. In 2004 and 2005, we traveled the length of the Valley, meeting with people in community centers and church basements. In more than 30 meetings, we spoke about our plans and goals for the winery.

"We want to work with anyone and everyone," Craig told the *St. Helena Star.* "Call us."

We meant it.

We listened and learned. One group emerged that appeared

to speak on behalf of the neighborhood. To meet the group's concerns, we significantly redesigned the project, including taking away a large berm, moving the warehouse, and reducing the height of the facility.

Then the county stepped in with different requirements, saying they wouldn't recognize the agreement we had made with the neighbors. More meetings. More negotiations. More architectural drawings. More design changes. More time—our project was delayed three years. And more money.

While the conflicts related to our Rutherford and St. Helena wineries were eventually resolved, others have proven to be more virulent. Developing a winery or a vineyard creates jobs, but it also encourages tourism, which is seen as a negative by some. Many of the people who protested our hiring Frank Gehry, for example, did so because they feared that the winery he designed would attract too many tourists.

People who talk about the risk of too many tourists point to the growing traffic in Napa Valley. They also note that more and more wineries are deciding to sell wine directly to the public, and blame the wineries for encouraging visitors and further burdening our roads. Much of this increased congestion, however, is simply due to a rise in the number of people who live here. Napa's population has surged from 79,000 in 1970 to 137,000 in 2015. In addition, as property values rise, fewer and fewer of the people who work in the Valley can afford to live here. The need for low, affordable, and even "normal" housing is high and the supply continues to decline. The reality is that there are many more people living and/or working in the area, and the infrastructure hasn't kept up.

That argument doesn't sway those who would rather not share "their" Valley with outsiders. Craig jokes that this very vocal anti-growth element in Napa would prefer that tourists fly over in helicopters and drop money rather than driving in and spending the night.

Everybody is here for quality of life, but how we all define our own quality of life differs. For some people that quality means no change. For some, change is okay, but not in my backyard. Most people want to preserve open space and to save trees, yet how do we balance this against a wine industry that increasingly wants to encourage winery visitors and plant more vineyards? We need to address the growing traffic problems, and that means creating new affordable housing for the local workforce, but in whose backyard? We need to allow some change, but if we lose the pristine beauty of the Valley we will have lost many of our tourists who are as attracted to Napa's natural beauty as to our wines. The key is to find the balance, but balance where?

So Napa remains in a situation where we all need to work collectively.

Our latest experience with trying to plant vineyards on a Napa piece of property we own is a good example of this bitter division and the difficulty in finding balance.

In 2005 we bought a 2,300-acre parcel of land zoned for agricultural use called the Miranda Leonard Ranch, a stunning property with some views that actually extend 50 miles to the Golden Gate Bridge. We hoped that the vineyard potential would match its beauty.

Because part of the parcel on which we wanted to plant vines was at a grade above 5 percent, we were required to do an Erosion Control Plan (ECP). The property is also large, so an Environmental Impact Report (EIR) was mandated.

EIRs, it turns out, are complex documents written by experts hired by the county and paid for by the landowner. The purpose of these documents is to analyze the property in order to ensure that the overall project will not adversely affect the environment. At the time, California guidelines specified that EIRs should take one year. Naively we didn't think that would be a big deal. As we write this ten years later, the county in its role as reviewing agency has yet to complete the final EIR.

We knew from the start that water would be an important issue. That didn't seem like it would be a problem when two water experts reported that we had one of the best water areas in the Valley, with a minimum of 1.4 billion gallons of water—and much more likely 3.6 billion gallons—under our property.

Our erosion control plans were similarly positive. It turned out that the development would actually *help* the quality of the city's water, which is downright uncommon.

We even had most every tree on the property over five inches in diameter (at breast height) measured and documented by hand. (The property is believed to have 235,000 trees on site.) We were preserving 90 percent of the trees. The housing development immediately adjacent, which was once part of our land, had preserved an estimated 71 percent of their trees. Nevertheless, our neighbors were decidedly displeased.

Despite our best efforts to responsibly develop the vineyard—which we named Walt Ranch after Kathryn's family—opposition mounted.

At the Napa County planning director's public meeting on November 24, 2014, tensions had rocketed to an all-time high. The hearing room overflowed with 80 to 100 people, many holding *HALT WALT* placards and wearing *HALT WALT* buttons. In July of that same year, the draft EIR, all 1,500 pages, had been released and groups quickly formed to oppose the project. Although no public meeting on a vineyard had ever been held, a decision was made to hold one about Walt Ranch.

The county had asked us to say a few words, so Craig led off, speaking for less than the three minutes allotted to each speaker.

He could have saved his breath. No one listened.

Tensions were high. One man came up to where Kathryn was sitting and leaned down real close. "You're the devil," he announced. "You're the devil."

The next morning, a dead bunny appeared in the entrance of our St. Helena winery.

Yes, Napa has considerable turmoil brewing within its beautiful borders.

Just like building a winery and planting new vineyards, developing housing in Napa Valley can be challenging and subject to community sensitivities. Since 2008, we've been in negotiation and discussion with county officials and the community related to the development of a mobile home park adjacent to our St. Helena winery. As we write, the project has yet to break ground after over seven years of effort.

Meanwhile, the core questions that divide the Valley remain unanswered. How do we preserve the natural beauty of the Valley, support the industry that supports Napa, manage tourism, and continue to sustain good jobs and infrastructure for our community? And can the Agricultural Preserve that the county adopted in 1968 be sustained in Napa Valley given the fact that wineries now increasingly want to sell direct to consumer, which means being tourist oriented?

There are some hopeful solutions being discussed. Making a substantial commitment to create affordable housing within the county would cut down on winery worker traffic. And a wine trolley funded by public and private money and initiatives—with a consistent schedule and regular stops at hotels, restaurants, and wineries—would further ease congestion. It would also help alleviate drinking-and-driving problems.

Like it or not, Napa Valley is a magnet that draws people to her. So the question we really need to be asking is, How do we grow in a way that honors the Valley's beauty and agriculture? This overly rigid protection of the Ag Preserve and agricultural zoning against any development—including agricultural cultivation, which is exactly what the Ag Preserve was designed to protect—invites litigation that ultimately could lead to the elimination of the Ag Preserve altogether. The truth is that by not allowing people to actually do agriculture in the Ag Preserve, extremists are putting the Ag Preserve in peril. And that could open the door to Napa very quickly becoming a bedroom community of San Francisco and nearby cities.

The Native Americans who inhabited this valley called it *Napa*, which means "land of plenty." Those of us fortunate enough to inhabit this land of plenty have an obligation. We simply must find a balanced way to share and preserve its bounty.

CHAPTER 12

The Great Recession and a Great Setback

While today we have the luxury of worrying about the survival of the Ag Preserve and the Valley as a whole, not that long ago we were worrying about our own survival. During the recession that began in 2007, premium wine sales fell off a cliff. Tasting room traffic in Napa slowed. The economy ground to a halt and with that so did our financial well-being. Restaurants could not sell the high-end wines they had in inventory, so they certainly were not buying more. In late 2007 and throughout 2008, everything just started to crumble. The following year, it looked like the industry was diving headfirst into a big black hole.

As challenging as our wine sales were, our other businesses (and investments) were worse. American Airlines, in which our family had invested heavily, was at the center of our financial woes, but we had others. To make matters worse, in 2005 we had gambled on increasing the quantity we made of our largest wine, our Napa Valley Cabernet Sauvignon. Whereas we made 5,000 cases in 2004, we made

20,000 cases in 2005. This represented an enormous increase in quantity of wine to sell in 2008 (the time the 2005 vintage was ready to be released) in the face of that year's contracting economy. So even though our sales grew, they did not grow nearly fast enough to move our additional inventory. Talk about adding insult to injury. We had lost lots of money before, but this time it was affecting our wines. We had to survive until we thrived.

CRAIG

I pride myself on being a tough guy who doesn't panic when things are rough. I believe that when stocks go down, you should not jump out if you fundamentally think you're in a good place. You should evaluate things on an objective rather than emotional basis. But it's hard to stay unemotional when everything you own is falling like a rock. Night after night, I'd sleep two, maybe three hours. I spent most of the hours between 10 p.m. and 4 a.m. sitting in front of the TV in my pajamas with a cup of coffee, a tumbler or a glass of wine, watching my family lose money in the different stock markets around the world. But I did not sell because that would mean defeat. I knew my investment was going to come back because it always did.

Well, the problem with that is that if you have debt, you're a fool. And I was a fool. But I'm used to debt, because that's leverage. Kathy always says that *Leverage* is my middle name. My parents didn't give me a middle name so I guess my wife did.

The whole economy in 2008 and 2009 just got worse and worse, and 2010 was no better. Sales—especially of wine—continued to be tough. Many of our friends were seeing some slowdown, but we were in a tailspin. While we were selling more wine than the year before, the growth in inventory far exceeded our ability to sell through normal methods. How do you sell lots of high-end wine in a disastrously down market?

In general you would think that excess supply means lower prices, right? Not entirely. Discounting wine can cheapen your brand for years to come. Especially with a brand as young as ours was in 2008, any significant discount could have tarnished our image. It also would have made a subsequent adjustment back to the "right," pre-recession pricing very difficult.

Kathryn, along with our sales team, hit the road, calling on every relationship we had to try to get people to buy our wine. We had three battles to fight. In addition to the economy, the 2005 vintage—which is what we were selling—was considered mediocre, and HALL was an unknown brand.

It's never easy to sell a wine that the buyer hasn't heard of. In difficult times it's worse. Wine buyers for stores and for restaurants will default to brands that are safe. So it quickly became a time to get creative.

By-the-glass restaurant sales—where the customer purchases wine not by the bottle but by the glass—became a good option. Here's how it works.

To entice a restaurant to carry a particular wine by the glass, the winery significantly drops the wholesale price. This dramatic price reduction is not visible to the consumer, so it doesn't impact public perception regarding the wine's value.

At the same time, the by-the-glass placement significantly increases the volume of wine sold. We sold a lot of wine this way in 2008. In short, by-the-glass programming is a win-win-win. Consumers can buy a glass of wine at a much lower price than they otherwise could, since the bottle has been discounted. The winery is able to sell overstocked wines in a larger quantity. And the restaurant makes a very nice profit. Even though we have a shortage of wine these days due to accelerated demand, we still do by-the-glass programming because it helps give the brand exposure to a new audience. This is especially helpful for a new brand like WALT. We want people to try our wine and this is a good way to encourage that.

To further help sales during the challenging market of 2008, we also made a few very specific deals with some very special retail friends. We sold a large quantity of the 2005 vintage to an upscale supermarket chain in Texas at a very deep discount. This can be a dangerous practice, as once you discount to a retailer they expect that lower pricing to continue. Bringing the price back up to "normal" levels is almost impossible. We did the deal because we trusted—and had a solid relationship with—this company. We believed that they would sell our wine quickly and be willing to buy from us at the normal price in subsequent years. That's exactly what happened. The chain did *floor stacks* (those large stacks of wine cases in the middle of the aisles that you have to walk around) of our wine in most of their locations. And they lowered the price to a very, very competitive price, but not so low that our image would be damaged.

This placement and the significantly reduced price allowed us to move a lot of our 2005 Cabernet Sauvignon in a very short period of time. Everyone was happy. The store made a good profit. Their patrons got a fabulous deal. And we cleared out the 2005 vintage without compromising future dealings with the store.

KATHRYN

We often say in our business that relationships are everything and that was certainly true in this case. The Texas retailer and our Texas distributor who worked with us in 2008 to move our 2005 Cabernet Sauvignon not only stayed with us in subsequent years, but they also returned to buying at our regular wholesale prices without a word. I saw the buyer this year at Premiere Napa Valley, a special annual tasting the Valley puts on for key buyers from across the country. He reminded me of our joint effort in 2008 and we both acknowledged that it had cemented our relationship. Reputation and real relationships are made in tough times.

The other way we moved a lot of our wine in 2008 was also relationship driven and downright serendipitous. I was attending an event in Dallas where Craig, who had been part owner of the Dallas Cowboys, and former Cowboys quarterback Roger Staubach, who had gone on to become a very successful entrepreneur, were being honored. Roger and I were seated next to each other.

"Tell me about the business," he said at one point during the afternoon.

After a great conversation, he asked if I would be interested in selling our wine to American Airlines, where he sat on the board. He proceeded to explain that he chaired a committee that encouraged American Airlines to buy from women- and minority-owned businesses. "If you're interested, I'll put you in touch with our wine consultant, Ken Chase."

Was I! The profile of people who drink quality wine aligns closely with people who fly, especially in first class. And the visibility of wines being poured during a flight is unusually high. As an Executive Platinum, almost-11-million-mile American Airlines traveler (who sits more often in 3A than in my home sofa), I was—and am—very familiar with the wines served on board. And although I was underwhelmed and hugely disappointed that, contrary to the George Clooney movie *Up in the Air,* no handsome captain comes out when you reach 10 million miles, I remain impressed by the knowledge flight attendants share about the wines they serve. So the possibility of an introduction to Ken, a Canadian who is extremely wine savvy and who has dramatically improved the wine selection aboard AA and other carriers, made my day.

I met Ken at a restaurant by Dallas/Fort Worth International Airport for lunch. We were joined by the woman who oversees the purchase of all beverages for American and by the woman who handles the minority purchasing program. The wines showed beautifully. It's a good sign when someone returns to the glass, re-tests the nose, looks carefully at the color, and then smiles as he sips. I watch for this behavior whenever I am presenting wines, and I saw it at lunch. Wow. Ken liked the wine. I could tell from his countenance that it was better than he thought it would be. He was clearly interested.

"If you want to buy 1,000 cases of wine, we can meet that level of request," I told him.

Thankfully, he jumped.

I can't think of a lunch I have enjoyed more than that afternoon with Ken and the American Airlines team. We talked about wines we love and why, and about the business of air travel—a topic that wound up impacting our family and our business far more than Craig or I suspected at the time.

Yes, even at the darkest times, there can be rays of sunshine. Time and time again we're reminded that this business of wine is so much about relationships. We make great wine, but we know many other wineries who do so, too. Very lucky for us, we also know Roger.

It took us more than the normal one year to sell through our 2005 Napa Cabernet Sauvignon. In the fall of 2009, as we prepared to release our 2006 Cabernet Sauvignon, we submitted the wine for review to the *Wine Spectator* critic James Laube. We were yet to have a wine rated over 90 points by the *Wine Spectator*, although with each vintage our wines were getting better. Despite submitting our vintage to wine critics, scores were not on our radar in 2009. It was all about surviving to see better days.

CHAPTER 13

Clouds with a Few More Rays of Sunshine

The economic downturn in 2008 and 2009 had an enormous impact on our budding wine business. And on our psyche. Special sales programs and support from friends helped to counter our slowing wine sales, but still the problem was huge. In that challenging economy, the extra inventory of our 2005 Cabernet Sauvignon vintage was simply not selling fast enough. To make things worse, we were in the midst of building an expensive new state-of-the-art winery at HALL St. Helena, and we were having serious difficulty finding ways to finance the cost of construction.

Traditional banks do not understand the peculiarities of the wine industry. That's what happened with ours in 2008. Making wine in a fully integrated way—owning and managing vineyards, running a production and sales facility, plus maintaining a high inventory as red wines must wait three years from harvest to sales—makes this business highly capital intensive. Our bank at the time—a middle market lender rather than a wine lender—just couldn't wrap its head around the complexities and needs of the wine business.

The clouds were pretty thick.

So we drew on Craig's capital-raising experience and a ray of sunshine started to appear—at least as far as the construction financing needs went. Craig had raised partnership money for investments while he was in college and for years continued to do so in his real estate dealings and other ventures. Now, 30 years later, we returned to Craig's former practices.

The good old days did not come back quite so fast. We tried our partnership offering twice in 2009 without much success. In 2010 we pivoted. That year we were joined by 54 new partners. We had found the right formula. The partnership took off. Add to that the fact that we found a new bank and our financing for the winery was suddenly secure.

And here's the best news.

Not only did we secure financing, our partners became our secret weapon. They have become an army of enthusiastic, supportive HALL and WALT brand ambassadors that extends across the country. Our investors each have business cards showing they're a partner in the winery. They share the HALL and WALT story and wines with their friends, at places they shop, and in restaurants they frequent. They recruit new wine club members and even other partners. Our team has now expanded from those of us in Napa to a great group of folks across the country. We all come together at the winery once a year for our annual partner meetings, which are fact-filled, wine-filled, and especially fun-filled weekends. As an added bonus, we have made many new friends, and many of our partners now have struck up new friendships with each other.

And our partners enabled us to complete the winery construction. However, the issue of slow wine sales in a depressed economy was a different matter.

In the summer of 2009 we needed some good news to give our little wine brand a push. Earlier in the year, we had received our first really good wine review from the *Wine Spectator*—93 points for our 2005 HALL Bergfeld Cabernet Sauvignon—as well as 92 points from Robert Parker for our 2005 Kathryn Hall Cabernet Sauvignon. Both were a big deal at the winery, but unfortunately both wines were already sold out, so the terrific scores did not help with sales. Nevertheless we all happily celebrated with a couple of bottles of wine.

And then. Bring out the sunglasses. In July 2009, the *Wine Spectator* critic James Laube awarded one of our 2005 Cabernet Sauvignons 95 points and three of our 2006 Cabernet Sauvignons scores of 96, 96, and 95 points. Most importantly, our 2006 HALL Kathryn Hall Cabernet Sauvignon (which was widely available) received 96 points and was described as "a big, dense wine, with currant and blackberry flavors and savory herb and earth nuances that provide a solid foundation."

We were over the moon that our hard work was being recognized. We both just started grinning. Although we felt as if we'd won the lottery, we'd actually been validated that our hard work had put us on the right path. Two months later, our 2006 Kathryn Hall bottle graced the cover of the *Wine Spectator*. Unbelievable!

That same year, Steve Heimoff of the *Wine Enthusiast* awarded one of its highest reviews of the year (97 points) to our 2006 "Exzellenz" Sacrashe Vineyard Cabernet Sauvignon. Shortly thereafter, the magazine highlighted the same wine as its 2009 #1 Cellar Selection wine *in the world*. Heimoff described the wine as having density "like a neutron star."

All of these 2006 wines that had attracted such positive attention from the wine critics were created by Mike, Megan Gunderson (who is today our associate winemaker), and consulting winemaker David Ramey, whose insights helped shape our wine philosophy.

To say that wine critics' acclaim matters to a winery is like saying that food reviews matter to a restaurant. Wine consumers have so many brands, wines, and varieties to sort through that they often need some guidance on emerging and established producers, not to mention which wines they should spend their money on. Wine critics have the advantage of tasting a wide breadth of wines and, as a result, are in a unique position to advise consumers about which wines to try. High scores from at least one of the wine review publications accelerate awareness about a winery while introducing the wines to a broader audience. So getting good wine reviews is important, and especially important when a winery is getting started.

James Laube of the *Wine Spectator* and Robert Parker of the *Wine Advocate* are two of the best known wine critics. But there are certainly others who are plenty influential— including *Vinous*'s Antonio Galloni, Steve Tanzer, and Steve Heimoff (who used to write for the *Wine Enthusiast*); *Wine Enthusiast*'s Virginie Boone; and the editor and publisher of the *PinotReport* newsletter, Greg Walter.

★　　★　　★

We have great respect for these critics and the jobs that they do. While some would suggest that being a wine critic sounds like a great job, where you sit around all day and drink and write about terrific wines, a lot of hard work is involved. Two wines can be equally exceptional and yet completely different. As a result, assigning ratings to hundreds of wines that all aspire to be at the highest level of quality is really hard. Add to that the fact that the wine critics must also characterize each wine in a descriptive and poetic way that sounds neither stilted nor hackneyed. Think about it. How many ways can you write about a Cabernet Sauvignon and not repeat yourself?

Here's how the tasting process works. When judging a wine, the critics evaluate:

- Appearance—color, clarity, and body.
- Aroma and bouquet—yes, there is a difference. There are actually two types of wine aromas. The second aroma, which develops only once the wine has been bottled, is called the *bouquet.*
- Taste—grape and other flavors, acidity, sweetness, bitterness, astringency, and balance.
- Texture—body/viscosity, mouthfeel.
- Finish—length, taste, balance, and body of the aftertaste.
- Overall impression—how all of those factors interrelate and harmonize.

Unlike most products, wine is a living thing that continues to evolve once it's bottled. When the wine is ready, it's taken or sent over to the *Wine Spectator* office in Napa Valley or to the offices of the *Wine Enthusiast, Wine Advocate,* or other critics. Delivering a wine for review doesn't mean that the wine is at its peak; the wines being judged are still young. But a wine critic understands that a wine that is just three years old will have growth. That's why they usually include advice in their review about when to drink it.

Over the years, we've gotten to know a lot of these hardworking wine critics, especially those who operate locally. As much as we like and admire all of them, we have a particularly fond place in our heart for the *Wine Spectator's* James Laube, Tom Matthews, and Marvin Shanken, because every June they throw a blow-out magnum party before the start of Auction Napa Valley. At the *Wine Spectator* party, you will see many of the top vintners in the valley. Invitations are hard to get since each winery only gets two invitations, so no invitation ever goes to waste.

Everyone brings a magnum to the party to share with their fellow vintners. There is not a shabby wine in the place. The party is held at a restaurant in St. Helena with a high-ceiling interior that makes the space feel like an Italian palace, and an outdoor area with metal tables, vines climbing the walls, a fountain, and lovely, aged brick floors. On the day of the *Spectator* party, this beautiful place is packed wall-to-wall with the who's who of the Napa Valley. Neither of us can think of any other time or place when there are so many fabulous wines and famous vintners and winemakers per square inch. It is an ultimate inside-Napa vintner experience for a group of people who are all about the wine experience. Thankfully, Uber finally arrived in Napa in 2014. If they had known about the *Wine Spectator* party, they would have come sooner.

We held our own private party in March 2010, when the *Wine Spectator* gave our 2006 HALL Napa Valley Cabernet Sauvignon a score of 94 points. While all the previously mentioned recognition had been important, this particular score really helped launch us forward because this was our most affordable and available Cabernet Sauvignon. After the rating came out, it felt like every wine store across the country wanted at least five cases of the wine (and some more) so they could introduce HALL wine to their customers. All of a sudden, instead of trying hard to sell the wine, we were actually allocating it.

There are wineries who do business that way all the time. If you are selling Château Latour, Domaine de la Romanée-Conti, or some of our cult wines here in Napa, you don't sell wine, you *allocate* production. The key to this sales strategy is both quality and scarcity, and the scarcity leads directly to higher prices for that wine. Our plan has always been different. We've hoped that by sourcing the best grapes, building state-of-the-art winemaking facilities, and working with the most talented winemakers, we can make great wines at a great value.

We resolved a long time ago that we were not going to produce our wines only to get high scores from wine critics. Our goal has been to make bold, concentrated, rich, and interesting wines that echo the places in which they are grown. Our wines must be different and reflect our own house style. Most importantly, they need to taste great. We also know that not every wine critic will appreciate our style of wines, but we are thankful that many love it.

Of course, just as glowing accolades help sales, the perceptions of the wine critic community can also work against a specific winery or vintage. Fast forward. In 2011, it rained late in the season, exactly when you don't want the grapes to get wet. Cabernet Sauvignon has thick skins, so it's usually impervious to rot. Not this time. The rains united the Valley. Everyone was talking about how best to contend with the weather, which was causing the grapes on the vine to spoil. One of our friends actually rented a helicopter and hovered over the vineyards to create massive air flow and help dry the wet fruit. We opted for a more hands-on approach.

Our director of winemaking, Steve Leveque, realized that the rot—or *botrytis* as it's known in the trade—had set in where the berry attaches to the stem. He also figured out that if you shook the vines vigorously, the affected berries, because they were compromised at that attachment point, would fall off. So he and Don Munk went into every vineyard we own and visited every grower we buy fruit from. At each vineyard, they demonstrated how hard to shake the vines. Then they tasted whatever fruit fell on the ground to see if the vines were being shaken too hard, which meant that perfectly healthy grapes had been dislodged. They ate thousands of rotten grapes that summer. But the process worked well and by the end of the season we saw more and more grapes throughout the Valley on the ground as more and more people adopted their own anti-rot techniques. When we sold the wine three years later, our approach prompted our "we shook it up" marketing slogan.

Due to this quick thinking and dedication, we were able to make some excellent wines that year. Unfortunately, the perception of the vintage was really poor. Customers and retailers told us, "We're just going to skip wines from 2011 and wait for the 2012s." To adapt, we developed a discount strategy along with incentives for our tasting room staff to spend more time selling the wine. Despite our efforts to move wine through our sales programs, sales remained slow. We could not buck the overall impression of the vintage. Then on August 14, 2014, a wine critic gave our 2011 Cabernet Sauvignon a 92 score—which was incredible for both the vintage and the price. The other wines that got similar scores cost ten times what our wine cost. Suddenly, our inventory problem disappeared. Just like that. Sales boomed.

The ripple effect didn't stop there. Top-notch wine reviews impact more than just wine sales. If you have positive wine reviews, your winery's reputation improves. As your reputation improves, it is easier to get great vineyards to partner with you and sell you their fruit. Vineyard owners want their grapes to go into great wines that they will be proud of. Of course, the better grapes you have to work with, the better your wines will be. So the cycle, once launched by the critics' acclaim, can perpetuate itself.

We were pretty ecstatic about those initial noteworthy scores and the ensuing orders that poured in. We still love that part.

CHAPTER 14

Doubling Down in Pinotland

By early 2010, the prospects for the future were looking up, so we decided to embark on a new project. For starters, we felt that opportunities had become available in the wine business—if you knew where to look.

One of our favorite wines has always been Pinot Noir. For selfish motives, as well as for the compelling and strategic reasons outlined below, we thought that we would try our hand at making Pinot Noir.

For starters, we reasoned that a Pinot Noir brand could build on programs already in place within HALL Wines. Besides, we had already invested in a state-of-the-art winery that would be perfect for the production of Pinot Noir. In fact, our HALL St. Helena winery was inspired by some of the designs of high-end Pinot Noir wineries from around the world. Some of the keys to top-quality Pinot Noir are the gentle handling of each berry, gravity-flow delivery to the tanks, and precision control of both the fermentations and aging. All that was already in operation.

Second, Pinot Noir tends to ripen earlier than Cabernet Sauvignon. As a result, we would be able to use the winery more than once in each harvest.

Pinot Noir is a less expensive wine than Cabernet Sauvignon, so we'd have a moderately priced line of wines to sell to a different type of wine enthusiast. Pinot Noir drinkers tend to be younger than Cabernet Sauvignon drinkers. They're geekier about wines and they spend a lot of time online, which is great for sales. These consumers would be new to us, and we wanted to connect with them.

Also our head winemaker had specialized in Pinot Noir before joining us.

We're not talking about Mike.

As HALL Wines had grown over the years, so had our original winemaker Mike Reynolds's responsibilities. Finally we realized that we needed him to relinquish his winemaking duties and assume the role of company president. So we looked for the best person we could find to lead what was already an awesome winemaking team that included Megan Gunderson, who has luckily been with us for years and now heads the WALT winery program, and Alison Frichtl, our enologist turned assistant winemaker. Steve Leveque, whom we found in 2008, had been the lead winemaker for six years at Chalk Hill, and a winemaker for 11 years at the Robert Mondavi winery, where he led the Pinot Noir production.

Not only had Steve proven himself to be a superlative winemaker when it came to Cabernet Sauvignon, he knew his way around Pinot Noir as well. Actually, that is an understatement of massive proportion. While at Mondavi, Steve had worked with more than 20 different clones and field selections of Pinot Noir from a myriad of different sites, soils, and terroirs. He didn't just *know* Pinot Noir. He excelled in Pinot Noir.

So at the beginning of 2010 we asked Mike to look for Pinot Noir brands that might be for sale since a number of wine brands were still in financial distress after the recession. Mike contacted all of the key people in the industry who buy and sell wineries, and we studied a large group of these, but nothing seemed like the right fit for us. After failing through the traditional channels, we broadened our search. Ultimately, Mike got a lead about a winery while watching a baseball game at the local Little League field. One of Mike's friends, who was doing some work for a winery that had not yet been offered for sale, connected him with the Roessler winery. (Napa still operates like a very small town.)

We purchased the Roessler Pinot Noir brand in August 2010. The purchase seemed logical on a number of fronts. There was no Roessler winemaking facility, so we didn't have to purchase that. We would just use ours. There were no vineyards. Roessler was simply a virtual winery with a tasting room and a following.

What the Roessler brand did have, which was the real value of the brand, was terrific relationships with the very top Pinot Noir growers along the West Coast, from Santa Barbara to Oregon. The Roessler brothers knew the importance of great vineyards. When it comes to Pinot Noir, that's downright critical. Pinot Noir is all about terroir, and terroir is really about how the wine expresses where that vineyard site is and the manner in which grapes were grown. Pinot Noir is substantially more sensitive to site than Cabernet

Sauvignon, which Steve found out while making Pinot Noir at Mondavi.

He had been working with fruit from a 50-acre property with at least 25 different clones. At the time, his favorite clone was called a Swan clone. He loved the Swan clone, and was pleased that it had been planted in different areas of that vineyard. Until he tasted the grapes. Just 50 yards down from Eastern Slope 9, his favorite block of Swan clone, the exact same clone produced downright terrible grapes. That difference would have shown up in a Cabernet Sauvignon, but in a much more muted, less dramatic way. But with Pinot Noir, while clones matter, the site trumps all.

As a result, Pinot Noir vineyards themselves become highly regarded. While you get some of that with Cabernet Sauvignon, it's nothing compared to Pinot Noir, where vineyards reign supreme. You'll often see appellations—the region the wine comes from—on a Cabernet Sauvignon label. With a Pinot Noir, the label will more often identify the actual vineyard in that appellation. That's because of how clearly the terroir is expressed in the final product.

Translation: If you want to make a great Pinot Noir, you need top-notch Pinot Noir terroir. A great Pinot Noir vineyard will typically exhibit the following site characteristics:

* Low yielding to create concentrations and personality.
* Low vigor—thanks to soils, weather (wind, for example), human-induced conditions such as water stress, etc.—to balance the low yield.
* Cool climate to retain freshness, nuance, and subtlety by preventing the grape from ripening too fast. In

California and Oregon, that boils down to proximity to the Pacific Ocean or, in the case of our WALT Browns Ranch Pinot Noir, San Pablo Bay.

- Rolling hills where the soil drains well instead of holding water.
- Lighter, loamy soils rather than heavy clay or overly rocky soils.
- Sustainable practices that provide longevity, healthy soils, and better vineyard expression.

Since Pinot Noir so profoundly reflects the vineyard it's grown in, you had better be able to procure grapes from the best vineyards around. But as we've seen, growers with great fruit want to align themselves with top-notch wineries that have proven themselves. Thankfully, Pinot Noir growers also honor long-held, solid relationships which we were lucky enough to procure with the Roessler brand and then maintain through the quality of Steve's Pinot Noir winemaking.

However, it didn't take long to realize that we had a problem. The Roessler name and story didn't have anything to do with us, so it didn't feel authentic. After selling wines for a year under the Roessler label, we felt this just didn't work. It didn't help that the name was difficult to say and even harder to spell. So we elected to rebrand our new acquisition.

But what would we call it?

We thought about HALL. The advantage of HALL was that we had spent ten years building up a brand under that name. The disadvantage was that it was a Cabernet Sauvignon brand.

So we picked a new moniker—WALT—Kathryn's maiden name. This one fit. We wouldn't be in this business but for the fact that Kathryn's dad had loved growing grapes. For us, WALT would become synonymous with great Pinot Noir.

Then we came up with a label and a logo. We tried to integrate the new name into the look that Roessler already had in place. Our mistake. It was not a good fit. After about two years, we realized that we needed to embark on the same kind of brand identity search for WALT that we had done years prior for HALL.

This time the process was easier, since we had been through this before and had a better sense of who we were. Still, there's a lot of subtlety that goes into the process. Working with Katherine Glass, who would later help us brand our Napa hotel SENZA as well as our Texas-based businesses, we designed a modern and fresh label that reflects the quality and style of wine inside the bottle.

As we write this in 2016, we are only a year into our new branding effort, but so far it seems to be going well. We are buying Pinot Noir vineyards and expanding our commitment to facilities and vineyards outside of Napa. The economies of scale for WALT and HALL—and the clarity of purpose for each—is working.

In the end, everything from the branding to the wines came together, meshing with the operation we already had in place. On the sales side, our team now walks into venues with WALT wines as well as HALL wines. On the production side, our talented winemaking team produces both the Pinot Noirs and the Cabernet Sauvignons using our existing tanks, which otherwise would have sat empty until the Cabernet Sauvignon harvest was in. So our whole system has become more efficient now that we can use it for WALT as well. Even better, the wonderful facility we have at St. Helena gives us unbelievable precision in the Pinot Noir wine-making process.

Most importantly, we can reach people who want a cost-effective, quality wine and bring them to Pinot Noir. Then maybe over time they'll also want to come in and know more about Cabernet Sauvignon. And vice versa with our Cabernet Sauvignon fans. We love that we can reach new consumers we would not have reached with HALL alone, and that we're building a family of people interested in different wines.

CHAPTER 15

Wine Has No Political Party

Wine brings people together. That's especially true in Napa Valley, where it trumps state and even national politics.

In the summer of 2002, we held a fundraiser in our home for then U.S. Senate Majority Leader Tom Daschle. We invited a group of our Napa friends along with some wine industry folks who weren't from Napa, including Ernest Gallo, who was then 95. Ernest came with a nurse who made no attempt to be inconspicuous. Dressed in a white nurse's outfit and rolling a portable oxygen tank, she stood right to the side of Ernest should she be needed.

Of course, we also invited Bob and Margrit Mondavi, even though we had heard rumors that Bob, then 91, and Ernest had fallen out in a big way many years prior and remained angry at each other. We didn't know the details and we didn't try to find out more. Frankly, we never thought it was our place to fret too much about internal Napa politics regarding who liked whom and who didn't speak to whom. We just knew that they had not hung out, or maybe even spoken, for years.

At the party for Tom, the two men found themselves in the same room. Both being advanced in age, they sat down on a sofa—interestingly, next to each other—along with Tom Daschle and started talking. Before we knew it, Bob asked Ernest, "Where did you land your helicopter today?"

"Over at the airport."

"You know, it is a lot closer if you land at my place," Bob said. "You'd be welcome to do that next time."

And so it went on and on, with the two giants of the industry renewing a friendship that had been sideways for years.

A newspaper photographer snapped pictures of Bob, Ernest, and Tom Daschle. The next day, the *St. Helena Star* ran a photo of just Ernest and Bob together. Only in Napa would two wine titans trump the leader of the U.S. Senate. This has nothing to do with party affiliation. National politics in Napa often doesn't.

During one of the earlier years of our time in Napa, Andy Beckstoffer, the very smart mega-vineyard owner who came to Napa from Virginia, invited us to an event for Congressman Mike Thompson that he was hosting along with Joseph Phelps Vineyards. At the time, we only knew Congressman Thompson on a very casual basis, although we would later become great friends.

Andy and Craig had met through the YPO/WPO (Young Presidents' Organization and World Presidents' Organization). Over the years, Andy has become the largest high-end vineyard owner in Napa and perhaps even in the country.

He's continued to grow and to do a great quality job. Although his son now runs most of the day-to-day operation, Andy's still very involved in making things happen in Napa Valley.

At the dinner he co-hosted for Congressman Thompson, Andy, who like all of us had drunk his share of wine, got up to give his toast.

"I don't know why I'm here or why I'm doing this," he announced in the Southern drawl he hadn't lost. "I'm a Republican and here I am giving $5,000 to a Democrat for his political action committee to get more Democrats elected. But I guess having the right guy on the job is more important, and Mike Thompson understands the wine business and understands what's important."

Victory after victory with large margins has shown that Mike Thompson, who coincidentally worked at the Napa Valley Co-op (now HALL St. Helena) after returning from Vietnam, really does transcend political partisanship. He has managed to do that because he's a phenomenal congressman who does a great job for all of his constituents. That's why he gets campaign contributions and votes from both parties. Mike represents an agricultural and wine community, and recognizes its needs.

More recently our friend and former Napa County supervisor, Bill Dodd, ran for and won a seat to the State Assembly as a conservative Democrat. Like Mike Thompson, he garnered support from both sides of the aisle.

Once in office, Bill honored Margrit Mondavi for all her work in support of the wine and food industry in Napa and throughout California. Both Democrats and Republicans stood and applauded when he presented her with a copy of the special proclamation.

We love it when Napa comes together like this, even though that's not always the case when it comes to local politics.

CHAPTER 16

Loving Napa

Despite homegrown political complications, we love it here. What's not to love about a region with an eclectic group of farmers, winemakers, marketers, business folks, artists, and more, all joined together by the appreciation of fine wine, and of living and working in this beautiful place? Oh, and awesome weather.

Even the dissension that seems to be growing within the Valley as we write this book comes from the shared desire to preserve and protect the beauty of the area. It is pretty amazing to be part of a community where people do not take its spirit for granted, and where in a matter of minutes we can be biking down the Silverado Trail (we can't wait for the wonderful new bike path that's coming to Highway 29) or hiking in areas that seem positively wild.

Most weekends, we'll get up early on a Saturday or Sunday, jump in the convertible with our two little Cavalier King Charles spaniels, and head toward our favorite trailhead. The dogs have done this so many times, they know exactly how the whole thing works. By the time we reach the outskirts of Calistoga at 8:30 or 9 a.m., they're ready to romp. The four of us hit the trail. As we wind our way up the hill and look south, the Valley stretches out in front of us like a sprawling vine. We keep climbing and before long we're so deep into the forest that we can no longer hear the sounds from the Valley or see anything but pines, laurels, and oaks, their branches intertwined and draped in vines. What a fantastic way to start the day!

That fact that Napa knows how to mix a nature-oriented lifestyle with camaraderie and great parties is a monster bonus. Truth be told, we still can't believe we get to attend some of these events. A birthday celebration in early April 2015, which Agustin Huneeus, whose nickname is *Cucho,* threw for his wife, Valeria, was one of the most amazing evenings we can remember. The party was, in true Cucho form, unexpected, natural, and joyous. We began with a glass of their Illumination Sauvignon Blanc, then proceeded to take a tour of the vineyard behind the house.

We climbed on his truck and drove up the mountain to the zenith where we could see the whole of the valley, from the vineyards in front of us all the way down to the San Francisco Bay. What a perspective! Frank Gehry would have loved it.

"This is where our son got married," Cucho said.

Some 10 minutes down another road we stopped again, this time at what Cucho describes as the most spiritual place on his property—a circular stone wall about 3 feet high that we were invited to sit on. As we approached we could hear a cello playing. Next came dinner on an island located in a body of water at the bottom of the vineyard. The natural birch table had been dressed with earthen plates and a burlap runner down its center. The effect was all earth tones, natural and beautiful.

After dinner we were invited to walk to the patio by the house for dessert and dancing to Latin music. All music moves the soul, but maybe Latin music does it best.

As we drove home we agreed that the party had been 100 percent Huneeus, and we would never forget it.

KATHRYN

This vintner life is still a fantasy turned real. After a long day at work, I am at times too tired to remember that, but the next morning the sun rises over the mountains that frame our Napa home and the fantasy starts again.

I do love the parties. My favorite party of the year is actually the one I give during the holidays for my women friends. It's great to hang out with women any time, but it's even better at this party where there's no business on the table other than wine and food, and the women are as interesting as they are diverse. The year we wrote this book, UC Davis Chancellor Linda Katehi, Napa Valley's fitness expert and trainer D'Nyse Chisolm, and San Francisco community leader Gretchen de Baubigny sat together and bonded. My sorority sisters from UC Berkeley college days mixed with our daughter Jennifer's Stanford business and law school friends. Winemakers, executives from both the Napa Valley Vintners and Grapegrower

CRAIG AND KATHRYN HALL

associations (two organizations at times in conflict with each other), educators from our tasting rooms, my Democrat activist buddies, and my most conservative vintner friends all just shared the joy of the season.

Unfortunately, Craig does not love parties as much as I do. We're a yin and a yang in a lot of things. He'll be the first one to tell you that I am a consummate party thrower and he's a consummate party avoider.

"I'm never going to another party," Craig announced to me in 2008.

For two years Craig got his way because we just couldn't afford to throw the parties. Finally I just couldn't stand it, especially since finances had improved.

"I am done with this," I told him. "You can just sit at home. I'm having the party and you don't have to attend."

He has come to our parties every year. And he has a good time whether he'll admit it or not.

The Napa social calendar extends well beyond parties. We may be located in the country, but local cultural opportunities range from BottleRock Napa Valley, a three-day music, food, wine, and brew festival attended by 100,000 (including us), to the Festival Napa Valley, which features ten days of classical music, dance, and theater events at a hundred Napa wineries. The Festival's 60-plus events also include art, fitness, and community programs along with the Valley's fine wines and cuisine. You want to run a 5K or 10K? Okay.

Meditation more your thing? That's fine, too. Of course, there are daily luncheons and dinners, followed by concerts featuring everyone from Herb Alpert and violinist Joshua Bell to the Russian National Orchestra. In 2014, conductor Carlo Ponti dedicated his performance to his mother, Sophia Loren (who was there as well), on her 80th birthday.

Then there's Music in the Vineyards, our summer chamber music festival, as well as November's Napa Valley Film Festival, with 125 independent films showing in Napa's four towns. And don't forget the ongoing performing and culinary arts events and wine-tasting programs available throughout the year.

Something about Napa, especially when coupled with the wine business, breeds a celebration of life. Every year, when the first truckload of grapes arrive in the winery, whoever happens to be present gathers on the crush pad. We welcome our interns who come from New Zealand, Australia, South Africa, and Mexico and other parts of Central and South America—generally wine students who are brought in by the Napa Valley Vintners association—along with our employees and any visitors. Then we bless the harvest, focusing on the cycle of life. Since every harvest is a continuation of the last, we take a bottle of the prior year's wine from the vineyard the grapes have arrived from and pour it into the grape bin. Finally, we pour more of that wine into our glasses and together we toast the new vintage.

At the end of each year's harvest, wineries—including HALL and WALT—throw parties for their employees. It's a way for everyone who has been doing little other than work and sleep (and not much of the latter) for six weeks to have a good time with their coworkers and families. Kids pop into the inflatable bounce house we rent, either before or after they've had their faces painted. Then the newly minted princesses and kitties and wild animals stuff their faces with guacamole and chips as they watch their parents dance to live bands that range from mariachis to rockers playing the latest hits.

There's nothing better than a party where everyone is there to celebrate, and that is just what happens when harvest is over. Those of us at wineries look forward to harvest every year, as it's the culmination of what we have been working toward all year. And once harvest is here, we look forward to it being over. And to the after-harvest party.

We also give a harvest party every year for our friends. This is a long-standing tradition for us. Kathryn started giving this party at her parents' vineyard in 1986. In the early days, she and her siblings would create a fire pit, bring in a band, and dance among the grapevines. We still have bands, but there have been some changes. Today we accommodate our female guests' high heels and keep everyone on terra firma over-looking the vines rather than in the middle of them. Plus, as we dance we watch our children and grandchildren next to us on the dance floor. Some of our guests—like Kathryn's cousin Louise Wright and her husband, Wayne, Liz Minyard and Paul Lokey, Rene and Sue Chouteau, Geralyn Cole, Jan Ritzau, Roger and Karen Eliassen—have come most every year since 1986. There is nothing like dancing under the stars all night with longtime friends, and each year this joy grows sweeter.

★   ★   ★

Nope, getting bored in Napa is definitely not a problem. Finding the time and energy to do everything, however, is another story altogether. And we haven't even started to talk about the charitable events that go on throughout the year.

CHAPTER 17

The Giving Napa

Napa Valley, and especially its wine industry, has a strong giving spirit. The ongoing array of fundraisers for our schools, hospitals, community organizations, and churches, coupled with the quality of wine donated and auctioned, has to constitute some kind of worldwide record.

This Valley truly believes in taking care of its own. Consider Auction Napa Valley, which has raised $145 million for local charities since it started in 1981. The idea behind auctioning off wine and travel donated by local vintners—along with other donations provided by non-winery partners like Bulgari and Riedel—is to take advantage of the Valley's worldwide reputation and then use that to enhance the well-being of the Napa Valley community. The event shares some similarities with the Hospices de Beaune charity in France, where Burgundy wineries raise money for their local hospital. But Napa has taken the idea many steps further. It is an all-American experience—open to all who will pay the price of admission, flamboyant, and—most of all—a lot of fun. Plus we all drink some of the Valley's best wines while raising money for our community.

Kathryn sits on the board's Grant Review Committee. She and her fellow committee members make recommendations to the full board about which charities deserve to receive funds from the auction proceeds. A few years ago, the board decided to go deep rather than broad, so the auction now focuses on two principal areas: children's education and community health. The goal is to make a significant impact in each.

To attract people who are prepared to donate serious money, the auction planners do whatever they can to make the experience special and unique. High bidders from the prior years are especially catered to. They're given fancy cars, such as Bentleys and Rolls-Royces, to drive over the course of the week. They're also wined (of course) and dined. We want them, and everyone else, to have a great time, to donate lots of money, to tell all their friends about this wonderful event, and to return the next year.

The festivities begin Thursday, with small private winery dinners in the company of winemakers and vintners for the title sponsors and those high bidders. These dinners are entertaining rather than formal. One year, our theme at HALL was the high school prom. Our staff dressed up as cheerleaders and pom-pom girls and the guests came in costume. Another year we hosted a Holly-Golightly-Breakfast-at-Tiffany's dinner. Many of the women wore hats similar to the beautiful brimmed hat we all associate with Audrey Hepburn. Theme parties like these help get our dinner guests in a party mood before they even arrive, and give us the chance to provide potential bidders with extra motivation by introducing them to a representative from one of the benefiting charities. As much as we want to raise money for Napa nonprofit organizations, however, the immediate purpose for all of us who host these parties is for folks to have a wonderful time and to take home memories they will happily share.

Friday is the barrel auction, where 2,000-plus people taste the special blends—still in barrels—that many wineries put together to be auctioned. Barrel wines are tasted inside the cellar of the hosting winery. Non-barrel wines are poured outside, under tents where local restaurants serve samples of their food. The mood is always very upbeat and the weather is generally sunny and warm, so it is a fun afternoon for all. Folks grab glasses upon entry and amble from table to table, tasting wine, talking, and comparing notes with strangers.

The year we wrote this book, the Auction Napa Valley Barrel Auction took place at HALL St. Helena. People strolled through the old stone Bergfeld building winery to taste wine and preview items that would be auctioned off the next day. They sampled wine from the 200 barrels that lined two floors of our new tank building, and checked out large, electronic display boards that showed in real time the top ten bids and corresponding barrels. At the end of the day, the winemakers whose barrel earned the highest price popped some bubbly as people cheered and confetti showered down on them.

At midday, we passed the word that people might want to make their way down to the tented great lawn at the side of the winery. They didn't know about the flash mob we had secretly been planning, in partnership with Festival Napa Valley.

Then, just past 1 p.m., clusters of "guests" from Volti Festival del Sole Chorale—positioned throughout the crowd with wineglasses in hand and looking, for all intents and purposes, like any of the other guests—broke into song. Conductor Ming Luke hopped up on top of a barrel and 40 musicians from the Festival del Sole Sinfonia, who were also scattered among the auction crowd, raised their instruments and began to play. As strains of Beethoven's "Ode to Joy" filled the air, the listeners, overwhelmed by the surprise of musicians all around them, smiled, laughed, and dabbed their eyes. Wow. Mission accomplished.

Saturday is the auction itself—always the most dramatic day of the week despite the fact that there are only 300 invitees, compared to close to ten times that many at the barrel auction. This event is always held in the afternoon. When the oversized white tent goes up on the expansive Meadowood lawn, it is as if the Great Gatsby has returned to life. Every auction chair brings new flair to the party. One year all the participating vintners marched into the tent in line carrying a magnum of their wine which the guests at their table would enjoy. It was pretty impressive.

Since the auction lasts for hours, folks tend to get pretty hungry after a while. The year the Chappellets chaired the auction, the family offered catered hamburgers for all. You should have heard the roar. Fine food served with wine pairings is great, but fancy food can get boring too. A hamburger never found such a welcome environment. But since this is the *Napa Valley* auction, the hamburgers were presented by servers who arrived in dramatic lines and placed the trays on all the tables in concert.

During the auction itself, folks sit at tables spread throughout the tent. Volunteers pass continually through the crowd carrying wire baskets full of various bottles of great wine. In addition, many vintners bring additional wines from their cellars. You can always see Garen Staglin and Tim Mondavi, among others, walking table to table pouring their wines for guests in what can only be described as an all-around festive environment.

The auction is conducted on a stage and televised on closed-circuit as well, so everyone can see everything no matter where they are sitting. Each year, vintner Fritz Hatton is one of the auctioneers. Fritz, who happens to be a professional auctioneer, knows not only wine but also the people in the audience, so his calls are personal and as a result very effective. His humor, twinkle, and impish demeanor make everyone smile and, perhaps more importantly, pay attention. He bounces around the stage, calling out people's names and talking about whatever crosses his mind, as well as, oh yes, the wine, or donated trip, or whatever he is auctioning off. It is a treat to watch.

When someone wins a bid, a huge hullabaloo ensues. Think horns and whistles and music and balloons, all brought to the winning table by an auction volunteer team with the offering vintner following right behind. Lots of fanfare and appreciation greet these folks who are bidding as much as six-figure amounts for their lot. With good reason. This money goes a very long way in our local charities.

The vintners are often at least as generous as the people who come to purchase. Every lot is donated by a winery. In addition, vintners often wind up being purchasers themselves.

One year Bob Mondavi offered his vest made of wine corks for auction. He came in wearing the vest and looking very uncomfortable. The vest did not move. It was bulky and, sorry, in our view not at all attractive. Koerner Rombauer of Rombauer Vineyards bought the vest for $95,000.

It was pure generosity of spirit. We have seen Koerner many times since, but we have never seen the vest again.

Molly Chappellet spontaneously added her sculpture to another auction lineup. Since her family had chaired the auction that year, she had melded her interests in gardening, vineyards, and art in the décor she created using wooden posts from old vine trellises. This last-minute donation was one more example of the generosity of the Chappellet family.

One of the most moving parts of the auction was started by John Shafer of Shafer Vineyards several years ago. John thought folks did not need to have a specific item to bid on. They might just want to give money to the Valley's charitable causes. So he launched the Fund a Need segment.

"Who will give $1,000 to Napa charities?" he asks. "Please stand and stay standing. Who will give $5,000? Who will give $10,000?"

And so it goes, up and up and up into the hundreds of thousands of dollars. By the time he is done just about everyone in the place is standing. In 2015, that segment alone raised more than $2 million.

John Shafer is a real motivator. He is so generous himself that he makes it hard to say no. For example, as the leading fundraiser for OLE Health, the affordable healthcare delivery service for the Valley principally serving farm and cellar workers, John has been tireless in asking people, including us, for help. When he asks, we—like most everyone else—respond.

"Lunches with you are very expensive," Kathryn once replied when he called to invite her out for a bite. "Perhaps you could just tell me what organization you are calling about because I know Craig and I would be glad to help."

The auction raises serious money for the community, which is why everything is geared to make this a true luxury experience. In 2015, the cost for the auction premier package was $3,000 and the VIP package was $15,000. People can also buy $500 tickets for the day-long barrel auction.

The auction certainly helps market Napa. Some people will come for the experience, but then get to know the quality of the wines and hospitality of the Valley along the way. Still, the community goal of the weekend is always front and center for every vintner.

That giving spirit certainly does not stop at the auction. Garen and Shari Staglin, who have also chaired the auction and who set the fundraising record the year they did, have raised and donated $880 million to charity since they began farming their vineyard in 1985. That's a lot of money—and doesn't count their work for UCLA! While their main cause is supporting research into mental illness, a fair share of all that money has gone to Napa organizations. The Staglins are a force of nature as fundraisers.

Wineries across the Valley regularly host and contribute to fundraisers for local school, church, and community groups. Perhaps some of the best wine values anywhere can be found at these events. HALL, for example, hosts several charitable events each year, including its Cabernet Cook-off, where 15 to 20 charities team with local restaurants to create a dish with Cabernet Sauvignon. The community attends, votes for their favorites, and a good time is had by all. Nickel & Nickel hosts the V Foundation wine auction to raise money for cancer research. Charles Krug hosts Hands Across the Valley, raising funds for organizations that fight hunger in the Valley.

That's just the start when it comes to wineries and charitable fundraising. Sutter Home has raised more than $900,000 to support the fight against breast cancer since launching Sutter Home for Hope in 2001. Humanitas Wines donates 100 percent of its profits to charitable organizations focusing on health, education, and affordable housing. The list goes on and on.

This generous Napa Valley tone was set by Bob Mondavi decades ago. A renegade who split from his family winery at Krug to start his own winery, he built Napa Valley into the world famous wine region that it is, while also shaping it to reflect his values.

CRAIG

Bob Mondavi believed that a rising tide lifts all boats, a notion that contrasts sharply with the competitive environment in most industries. When we first came into the wine business, I couldn't get over how people here were so helpful to each other as an industry.

"We're not competing with each other. We're competing with the world," Bob used to say. "Let's figure out ways to help each other and make the best wine in Napa Valley."

Bob really *was* the wine industry and this philosophy molded his approach. He not only helped newcomers, he welcomed them as well as their ideas. He was the key glue that held everybody together.

As a couple, Margrit and Bob not only made Napa Valley, they were the soul of Napa Valley. We miss Bob now that he's gone and continue to treasure Margrit. We will always remember that their friendship and their support filled our lives with joy, and helped us through some dark times during the planning phase of our St. Helena winery. And for that we will be forever grateful.

CHAPTER 18

Introducing HALL
St. Helena

We had been in mid-construction of the new St. Helena facility, doing the redevelopment in stages, when the Great Recession hit hard in 2008. While we had completed the revamp of the temporary tasting room, the demolition of the outdoor tanks, and the construction of the fermentation tank buildings, the barrel storage buildings and the parking lots were still under way. Despite our money woes, we had to finish those because we had entered into construction contracts. The rest—including the new hospitality area, as well as the restoration of the 1885 original winery—would all have to wait until we had financing.

In light of the financial setbacks we had suffered and the fact that we didn't have a workable roof that actually held up, we reluctantly concluded that we would have to part ways with Frank Gehry. We opted for a young, talented, and enthusiastic architect named Jarrod Denton. In 2006 Jarrod had been employed in the architectural office of Jon Lail, the local architectural firm working with Gehry. Jarrod had moved on since then, starting with a partner: a new Napa Valley–based firm called Signum Architecture. While Jarrod was certainly not well known, we really liked his style and had great faith in his ability to create a winery we would love.

Our goal remained the same: to meld modern architecture, art, and nature—along with the experience of the winemaking process itself—into a backdrop for tasting wine. The plan was to present our visitors with a sensory feast.

We also wanted to restore and celebrate the 1885 historic winery and acknowledge the winemaking tradition of the Valley. Over the years, the 5,200-square-foot building had been part of the warehouse. After we bought the property, we used the downstairs portion as a wine lab. We couldn't use the upstairs. The roof had not withstood the test of time or weather, so the upper part of the building had essentially crumbled away. As a result, once we decided to restore the old winery, we had to redo most of the second story. Our favorite part was the floor, which still had the original tray that funneled freshly made wine into the barrels that were taken away by a horse and buggy. We wanted the rest of that second story to look just like it had when wine was still being poured through that tray.

With no blueprints to consult, we had to reconstruct (and earthquake-proof) the handmade wood and stone structure based on a single photo that was also a little worse for wear. The building now looks almost exactly the way it did 130 years ago.

Jarrod then designed a winery that was visually exciting, highly functional, and cutting-edge from an environmental standpoint.

"Wow, I can't believe that I did this," he said one day, with a shake of his head as he was walking through the winery after its completion in 2014. He seemed truly surprised.

We weren't surprised. We knew he could do it. But we sure were excited about the results, especially when HALL St. Helena was awarded the first LEED (Leadership in Energy and Environmental Design) Gold certification for a California winery.

We try to be green. Our vineyards are farmed organically. The costs are higher, but this decision is non-negotiable. In 2009 and 2010, when we were not sure if our wine business would survive, we asked our department heads to propose budget cuts. Our vineyard manager Don Munk's numbers showed that we could save upwards of $250,000 a year in farming costs if we farmed using more traditional methods. The savings would have been swell, but the team collectively just couldn't go there.

The St. Helena winery actually holds two LEED Gold certifications. Developed by the U.S. Green Building Council (USGBC) and considered the nation's preeminent building ratings program, the LEED rating system provides a framework for green building design, construction, operations, and maintenance standards.

To meet the requirements to become LEED Gold–certified, we added many sustainable design elements and practices including:

- Radiant floors—Cold or warm water runs through the floor slab to control temperature. This gives us an energy-efficient and stable storage and production environment, which helps with precision winemaking.

- Solar energy—Solar photovoltaic cells provide more than 35 percent of the winery's energy needs. Approximately one acre of solar panels spans the St. Helena winery roofs. As a result, the winery sells energy back to the grid.
- Local building materials—More than 10 percent of materials used to build the facility were extracted, harvested, or recovered—as well as manufactured—within 500 miles of the winery.
- Recycled building materials—More than 10 percent of the materials used were made with recycled content.
- Water conservation—The winery landscaping consists of drought-tolerant plants that reduce the demand for irrigation by more than 50 percent. In addition, all of the landscaping and vineyards are irrigated with recycled water. This, including the reuse of water from wine production and low-flow water outlets, reduces the need for water by 40 percent.

Landscape architect Jim Burnett, from Houston and San Diego, created a variety of spaces for guests to enjoy tasting wine, with the valley and hills as a gorgeous backdrop. Many of these spaces are also great for art.

Patrick Dougherty—an artist whose large-scale work made from willow branches is suggestive of nests and lairs—created his "Deck the Halls" installation in Jim's olive grove. Patrick's creations are group efforts. He has the vision and then volunteers help bring that vision to life. Over a three-week period, Patrick ran around like a gloved conductor interweaving willow branches and twigs together, and telling dozens of people, including us, how to do the same and where to shove the ends of the willows into the ground. Many on our winery team will show you today with pride the arch or willow wall they constructed.

By the front entrance stands John Baldessari's 12-foot-tall "Camel (Albino) Contemplating Needle," a 2013 fiberglass, aluminum, stainless steel, and acrylic sculpture that alludes to numerous religious texts including the Midrash, the Quran, and the Bible. People love the camel and, unfortunately, also love to try to ride it. So, our hospitality team put up a sign: *Camel rides on February 29 of odd years. Until then, please refrain from disrupting the needle contemplation.*

At the back end of the winery grounds lies an infinity-edge reflecting pool created by decades-long Texas friend, Jesús Moroles. Early on during the construction of the winery, before we had done much landscaping, we were standing with Jesús in the 1885 Bergfeld building, looking out over the vast area of dirt.

"What about if you did a big reflecting pond with my stonework and when you looked down the glass of the water reflected the mountains?" he asked. "I've never done one quite like that before, but I'll do it for you guys."

Sold!

A small sign beside Jesús's reflecting pond reads *Lifeguard not on duty.* One visitor returned wearing a bathing suit and swim mask. Wonder what our guests on the tasting room balcony that overlooks the water feature thought that day.

Inside, as you walk up the stairs to that tasting room, you'll find a piece by Peter Wegner made out of 24,000 index cards.

Can you imagine creating that? Peter and his team were here for three full days installing all those cards section by section. Unbelievable.

Just beyond Peter's work is "Exploded View (Expanding)," a video art piece by Jim Campbell made out of 1,728 LED lights in which birds seemingly fly through at random. Every 20 minutes or so, a large blackbird flits across the lights. It took a long time for Jim to find the appropriate spot for this piece, as there are so few winery spaces dark enough to show the lights. We love where it is now. It's the first thing you see when you reach the top of the stairs, and it remains the piece that most people cluster around.

In the tasting room just beyond, Spencer Finch's glass panels suspended on almost invisible wires reflect the light outside as well as the colors from the large geometric mural he created along the back wall. Spencer, who was commissioned to do a piece for the 9/11 Memorial in New York, has created a work that reflects how the light in the Valley changes throughout the day and throughout the year.

Like wine, art speaks without saying a word. Our hope is that the winery structures, grounds, wine, and art all add layers to the experiences of our guests. As our friend Gina Gallo said many years ago, "There's no such thing as a beer moment, but there are wine moments." Our goal is to make those wine moments unforgettable—whether you visit us in person or on the Internet.

CHAPTER 19

Delivering in a New Way

"People will never buy wine online," one of our key people stated ten years ago. He was adamant. "They don't do that. It will never happen."

He was right about the fact that people weren't purchasing wine online at that time. Winery websites were originally information sites. You could visit a winery's website and find out where the winery was located. You could learn about its philosophy, its owners, the winemaker, what wines it sold, and maybe what tours were offered. You might even have been able to buy some wine, although that was pretty rare until just a few years ago.

We decided early on that we would bet on the Internet as an important sales and marketing tool. We intended from the start to grow our direct-to-consumer business. By 2003, we began to believe that the Internet would be key. That same year, we started putting information online and staffing our marketing department more heavily than was warranted for a winery our size. Then we proceeded to stumble a lot.

We hope our gamble will pay off as people's buying habits shift from brick and mortar to online. While all our sales are growing at a rapid rate, we think our online sales could be our fastest growing area in the next few years. Once again luck has played a part—this time in two ways.

Over the last six to eight years, as technology has improved so have the interstate shipping laws regarding wine. The rapidly shifting laws now allow online commerce in a way they didn't when we bought the former Napa Valley Co-op property in 2003. Before 2005, for example, wineries in California were precluded from shipping wine to most places outside of the state. Little by little, these restrictions have eroded.

Online commerce and direct shipping restrictions still vary from state to state. For example, we can only send a certain number of cases per year to a single Texas address, and as of this writing we simply cannot ship wine to Pennsylvania. Still, the changing laws are changing the way we do business, and our focus continues to shift from distributors to the consumers themselves.

Not that long ago we, along with every other vintner, hoped that a salesperson at any wine store on Main Street would have tasted all the wines the store carried, have the ability to discern one from another, and tell their customers why our wine was so good. This knowledgeable store salesperson is still invaluable, as third party validation is still such a powerful persuader. But today we can also rely on other third parties—the other people in cyberspace who have tried our wine and are willing to share their comments about it. In addition to the in-store sales team, today we look to websites and blogs, such as *Haute Living, 7x7,* and *Vinography,* and to anyone in the anonymous digital world willing to take the time to review our product on our website—which has a place where anyone can leave a comment and rate any of our wines—or anywhere else. With today's technology, we can hopefully rely on other messengers in addition to that guy in the wine shop.

A website used to be like a corporate brochure, with visitors starting at the beginning and ending at the end. Sure, they could skip around, but it was a one-size-fits-all approach with an informational rather than transactional focus. Now e-commerce can come to the wine business in general—and to HALLwines.com and WALTwines.com in particular—in the most personal way. If you are a member of our wine club, when you shop online you will see your special lower pricing rather than the price offered to the general public.

We will also communicate to you in ways tailored to your interests. If you recently purchased our Howell Mountain Cabernet Sauvignon, we will send you other emails about single vineyard Cabernets in that price range. Online marketing can be at least as personal as talking with your wine salesperson in your favorite wine shop and it's definitely more convenient. If you only like 90-plus-point wines, we are going to be sure to tell you about our newest 90-plus-point rating. If you buy red wines, you won't be on our list of people to reach out to about our Sauvignon Blanc. If you prefer Pinots with bright red fruit, we will send you information on our WALT Clos Pepe before we tell you about WALT Shea vineyard. We use this information to customize our messaging and to reach out to consumers with new products and offerings that will be well received.

Social messaging can be just as customized as your website experience. We know that our Twitter followers are more likely to be interested in scores than our Pinterest followers, whose varied interests range from food, to weddings, to culture. This kind of information permits us to tailor both our offerings and our messaging, and not waste our customers' time on something they're not interested in.

The technology already exists today to make our customers' online experience at least as personal as talking with a wine salesperson in their favorite wine shop, and a whole lot more convenient. At the same time customers may want to chat online or over the phone when they have questions, so we will offer that too. Our goal is to provide service in the specific way that works for all our customers.

We hope the technology we've adopted customizes and maximizes the experiences of our customers, whether in person or on the Internet. And we'll keep on trying to do it better as we gain experience, because, let's face it, all this is pretty new to us.

Wine came late to the online shopping party for a number of reasons. As we've discussed, wineries have to be compliant with the laws of each state they ship to, which adds a huge legal complication. In addition, wine is heavy, which makes it expensive to ship, and it can spoil, which makes it challenging to ship.

Even so, wine is a natural fit for online sales. If people will use the Internet to buy tennis shoes without trying them on, cantaloupe without smelling it, and a sweater without touching it, buying wine online is a no-brainer. After all, it can't be touched, smelled, or tasted until you've purchased it anyway. In addition, there are ways to use today's technology to make an online relationship far different than you might think. For example, people can go online and watch our harvest live from the perspective of the crush pad. Our winemakers and wine educators can discuss our wines in real time on the website and potentially help guide consumers through an online purchase. Eventually, just like shoes, people will be able to send back anything they've bought online that they don't like, thereby ensuring 100 percent satisfaction.

Virtual consumer relationships are growing and social media is gaining in importance by the day. This is true for almost all retailers, but for wineries, which have traditionally been at the mercy of a complex and impersonal distribution system, what technology has done to directly connect wineries to consumers is a sea change.

Broadcast used to reign supreme in terms of advertising; now influential HALL and WALT fans saying positive things about the brand create the buzz. Think about it. What sways you more, a message paid for by a company or a favorable mention by a third party? So our advertising and marketing increasingly revolve around social media. A visitor who posts a picture taken at the winery, or adds a hashtag to something winery related—whether #LittleBunnyFooFoo, #HALL, #WALT, #crazygoodcabs, or #pinotland—creates a brand moment for that consumer and the people in his or her social networks. Today we are building our business by creating millions of quality brand moments with consumers that result in long-term advocacy and loyalty.

Twenty years after breaking ground on our Rutherford vineyard and a year after the grand opening of our St. Helena winery, we sell more than two-thirds of the wine we make direct to consumer. We like being able to establish a personal relationship with the people who like our wines. Regardless of all the exciting changes in technology, this is a very personal business.

While we love direct relationships, we also want to be available in restaurants that folks who enjoy our wines frequent. Our distributor partners in all 50 states and many countries around the world make that happen. We are really grateful for some long and, we hope, mutually beneficial relationships. Interestingly, our direct relationships have helped create restaurant demand, or *pull-through* as it's called, which helps our restaurant and distributor partners. That's all good. Meanwhile, we will continue to try to establish a relationship with our supporters online. Our goal is to encourage more people to experience our wines, not just in this country but around the world, and the best way we know to do that is through the Internet.

Hopefully, many of our online visitors will want to join our wine club. Wine clubs are not for everyone, but they are a great advantage for some and are a great way for us to get to know our public. Club benefits include access to small production wines, VIP treatment and benefits at the winery, and discounts. The clubs also give us a chance to share a little of the wine country lifestyle. Each year, for example, we have our WALT Lobster Feed in the middle of one of our Sonoma vineyards and the HALLiday at Our House party in our home. At these events and many more throughout the year, we all simply get to have fun. The secret to the success of any wine club—and to online sales in general—boils down to relevant and consistent person-to-winery contact, no matter where our current or prospective followers live.

Our competition is less the guy down the street than it is a vintner in Bordeaux or Argentina or any of the other top wine-producing areas around the world. So instead of worrying about how we're stacking up against some of the Valley's other wineries that make top-notch Cabernet Sauvignon, we're more concerned about promoting Napa to drinkers in New York, in France, in Australia, in China. We'd like them to drink more Napa wine—hopefully ours, but if not, then one of our neighbor's—so that one way or another more folks will understand just how memorable a wine from Napa can be.

Much has changed since we began our adventure in Napa. What hasn't changed is the importance of relationships. The wine business is a people business, one in which we sell a luxury product based on a reputation built slowly and through personal experience. We hope we understand the business better, and we try to market our wine today with more nuance. We have learned a lot about making wine, and we're always looking for ideas and/or technology that will help edge us to better and better quality. But nothing beats being part of the winemaking process.

CHAPTER 20

Tank Walk

The clock showed 6:30 a.m. Even though it was still dark outside and she had slept just five hours, Kathryn forced herself out of bed. It was harvest season and grapes had hit the tanks. So it was time for the daily tank walk.

During the three-month-plus harvest, our winemakers open up the spigot at the bottom of each and every tank each and every single day to monitor how the juice within is progressing and help its evolution. They'll visit some tanks multiple times per day if further action or time-sensitive decisions need to be made. During those recurring tastings, the winemakers decide how they're going to handle the fermentation of each tank at that particular time in order to capture the wine they're aiming for. They may increase the temperature, decrease the temperature, or expose the juice to oxygen to soften the tannins. They'll check sugar levels and decide how best to bring the juice in contact with the *cap* (that top layer of grape skins, stems, and pulp) to achieve the perfect level of extraction when it comes to the wine's flavor, tannins, and aromas. Since each vineyard—and each block within each vineyard—is different, each tank requires a different approach and every tasting provides a unique opportunity to build the wines. That's why there are never any days off during harvest for our winemaker Steve Leveque. He can't afford to miss a single tank walk.

We love joining in on the tank walks whenever we can, although Kathryn goes along far and away more often than Craig does.

Not much need for makeup, Kathryn told herself as she put on eyeliner, shadow, mascara, and blush in anticipation of the early tank walk. *Definitely no lipstick or gloss. We'll be sharing wineglasses in 30 minutes and lipstick stains on the communal glass are not cool.*

She threw on her jeans and pulled on the dark blue rubber Chanel boots she adores—practical but with a little flair from the two little rubber flowers on each side. *Maybe someday when I grow up I can wear regular shoes on a tank walk, but not yet,* she thought. *I still can't spit well and in a line.*

Her spitting may not be up to par, but her solution to the problem works.

"I love your boots," one of the cellar interns from Argentina had exclaimed during the prior day's tank walk.

The comment both flattered and impressed Kathryn. She likes to see flickers of style in the tank room, just as she enjoys looking up at the art we have installed above and around the fermenters as she and the winemakers work their way through the morning. As she moved on to the next tank, she made a mental note to find out the girl's name.

Although we make wine in both the Rutherford and St. Helena facilities, this tank walk would start at St. Helena since that winery has many more tanks to go through and more decisions to be made. Opting to leave the top down on the car during the drive that takes just nine minutes at the crack of dawn, Kathryn felt herself waking up thanks to the sharp freshness of the wind. She inhaled deeply, taking in the vinous and slightly sour fragrance that permeates the valley during harvest when all the wineries are fermenting.

A TV journalist would be walking with them that morning, a primary reason behind the eye makeup. Michiel Vos, a Dutch TV personality and journalist living in the U.S. whom Kathryn knows through his mother-in-law, Leader Nancy Pelosi, was doing a story on Napa Valley. Michiel and the cameraman were already at the winery when Kathryn arrived. Together the three headed to the lab to get their tasting glasses and then went in search of Steve Leveque, our director of winemaking, Megan Gunderson, our assistant winemaker, and Gabriel Valenzuela, then our cellar master. Vintners get a lot of attention and winemakers are the movie stars of Napa, but this train wouldn't even have run much less started on time without Gabe.

By 7 a.m., the group that would participate in the morning tank walk stood in front of the first tank. Steve and the other winemakers never just rely on their fantastic memories about what's been done to the wine in each tank and how it tasted the time before. As they progressed from the first tank to the one next to it to the one next to that, they reviewed the running record of how the juice in that tank had been handled. The date it came in. The Brix (measure of sweetness) level. The temperature throughout each day and how that translated to a change in the Brix or in taste.

We hold the juice at 50 degrees Fahrenheit to discourage

fermentation and to allow for the extraction of flavors and other qualities that stem from leaving the skins on the juice before fermentation begins. Once we start fermentation, we have different options for flavor extraction. For the Pinots, we generally keep the temperature in the 50s for four to six days. For the Cabernets, the extensive cooling process can last four to ten days. When we start allowing the temperature to rise, which it does naturally during the fermentation process, the Pinot ferments quickly and in big leaps. Cabernets are slower. In either case, the juice must be tested several times each day to make sure the process is continuing as Steve wants.

The group began to taste, opening a small bottle drawn by an intern an hour earlier from the first tank. They poured a small sample in each person's glass. Kathryn and the rest took a sip, let it linger on their palates, and then spit it out—Steve into the floor grate 2 feet away, and Kathryn, although she aimed at the same place, onto her boot.

Discussion then ensued about what to do with this particular tank, mostly a back-and-forth between Steve and Megan who, at that point, had worked together for six harvests. Although they are not always in agreement, we both love watching their communication with each other.

"Do we keep the temperature as it is?" "Is the flavor developing as we want?" "Is it ready to start the fermentation process?"

Within a couple of minutes, a decision had been reached and the directives marked on the instruction card for the cellar master and his team to execute. Then the group moved to the next tank.

At no time was the wine assessed qualitatively. That

doesn't happen until the blending season. So we can have a truly special wine in the making, like the Exzellenz Cabernet Sauvignon we had made three years prior, but have no idea that it will vault us into downright rarified company. (That shocker would hit just a few days after this particular tank walk.)

In a dining setting you start first with the white wine then go to the reds, but not in a tank walk. The tank walk crew got to our Sauvignon Blanc after about 90 minutes. This is when the communal glass comes in. We clean all the red wine out with a blast of Sauvignon Blanc that we pour from one glass to the next until the last person tosses it out.

Once the glasses were clean, or as clean as they'd get on a tank walk, a real sample of Sauvignon Blanc was poured into each glass.

Yuck! Kathryn said to herself after tasting the juice. Sauvignon Blanc is tough during the fermentation process. It's sour and has a Heineken beer quality (remember a weed is a rose out of place), with little redeeming quality until the end.

Kathryn steeled herself for the rest of the tanks that she'd have to get through. One of the Sauvignon Blanc samples, however, surprised her. It was lovely, its Muscat clone giving a beautiful illusion of sweetness and fruit that all the tasters loved. We bought the fruit that had gone into that particular tank from our neighbors across the street, the Heitz family. What a wonderful vineyard. Hopefully, they'll continue to sell to us.

By now, Michiel, despite his knowledge of wine, was looking a little bit bored. The morning's tank walk had taken a little over two hours, even though we were only three-fourths of the way through harvest at this point, which meant that about half of our tanks were still empty. A week later, it would take more than three hours just to get through the tanks at St. Helena, before driving up to Rutherford to work on those wines.

After the last tank, the small group walked out of the tank room and into the light, always one of Kathryn's favorite moments of the day. Having walked sleep-deprived into the tank room when it was dark and cold, she emerged with the bright, beautiful California sun shining in her eyes.

I love it, she said to herself. *Let the day begin.*

Most winemakers around the world follow their own particular recipe that dictates how they handle the tanks during fermentation. They'll taste every day, but they don't usually make any substantial modifications. At HALL Wines and WALT Wines, every tank walk presents a unique opportunity to build each one of our wines day by day. The ultimate goal is to pull everything good out of the grape and leave behind everything we don't want, thereby creating a perfectly textured, balanced wine.

CHAPTER 21

Making the Best Wine We Can—for Your Inner Geek

Over the last ten years, technology has changed the wine industry more than it probably has in the last 1,000 years. And up-and-coming technology will enable us to make even better use of great winemaking artistry and great fruit. Take the new software program being developed by InnoVint to help wineries' admittedly archaic production work flow. Instead of just jotting down notes or using Excel spreadsheets, cellar and vineyard teams will be able to use the software to track information in all areas of production. As work orders are developed and carried out, the information will be recorded on handheld devices. That same kind of detail will be recorded for every phase of growth and production. Winemakers will eventually be able to instantly know exactly how a vineyard block was watered in a particular year, how much fruit that section produced, and how it was processed.

In short, this new software will allow the winemaker to

see at a glance everything that has impacted each individual barrel of wine produced. (You'll understand in a moment just how complicated that can be.) Whatever information winemakers and vineyard managers need will be right at their fingertips, allowing them for the first time to effectively coordinate their efforts. This kind of high-tech approach to production is certainly not new in most industries, but it's revolutionary in ours. Better information will mean better results and at a lower cost. Save money and improve quality—why not?

CRAIG

InnoVint's Ashley DuBois went to UC Davis and graduated from the same enology and viticulture programs Mike Reynolds attended years earlier. She used her skills to become a winemaker, but left the wine industry to go into the tech world. Then she figured out how to put together her two areas of interest and expertise. She decided to start InnoVint and develop state-of-the-art software for wine production and vineyards. When we first met, Ashley and her partner and cousin, Andrew Headrick, had spent three years developing their software product, which is still a work in process.

Ashley is the real deal. We believe she and Andrew can dramatically change winemaking for the better. So we provided Ashley and Andrew with capital to help them take their product from concept to reality. As of this writing, that work in progress is finding good success with smaller wineries. From our perspective, this is the type of new technology that will help dramatically improve the quality of wine for everyone.

Despite this kind of game-changer technology, some of the old ways remain the best. Take gravity-flow winemaking, a traditional method dating back as far as 5,000 years, where gravity triggers the grapes to flow into the tanks. Grapes falling into the tanks due to gravity, rather than being pumped, is far better for the wine. Gentle processing, where grapes are not prematurely broken up or bruised, allows for maximum depth and intensity of wines. It also reduces or eliminates bitter, harsh tannins by keeping the skins intact and the seeds, which can impart an under-ripe taste especially when ground up by a pump, safely encased within the berry.

This is part of the difference between high-end winemaking and volume winemaking, which always pumps the grapes. While there are several different types of pumps that people use in the wine industry, none of them are gentle. That means that the winemaker has to then cover up the harshness of the tannins from all those shredded skins and ground seeds by manipulating the wine with additives. And that distracts from our goal of letting the vineyard attributes and personality shine through in the wine.

While the core of how wine is made today has remained the same for thousands of years, very recent technology has created powerful tools to raise the quality of wine. The key is to find the sweet spot—to meld technology and tradition. So just like our Rutherford winery, which juxtaposes a traditional old Austrian brick cave with a Star Wars–like fermentation room, and the St. Helena winery, which contrasts the historic Bergfeld building with our state-of-the-art production facility, our winemaking goals can be summed up in three words: *Tradition meets innovation.*

These days, for example, we don't rely on the human eye to guarantee that only the finest grapes go into our wine. Once the fruit has been handpicked in the predawn hours to ensure that the berries are cool and firm, it gets evaluated by our harvest team. Each bin of fruit is elevated above the hopper. The clusters are then gently ushered onto a sorting table where we go through them by hand to remove imperfections and *MOG* (Material Other than Grapes). The fruit then goes through an oscillating destemmer. Although fairly common now, it was one of only six such precision machines operating in the Napa Valley when we purchased it. This state-of-the-art technology gently removes the fruit from its stem, allowing the whole berries to spread evenly across a conveying table. Once on the conveying table, the individual berries are optically sorted.

Developed in France and launched in 2008, the 10-foot-long sorting machine optically assesses the quality of each grape that comes into the crush pad. Here's how it works: With every batch, the winemaker finds 100 to 200 of the best berries and feeds them into the optical sorter. The fruit passes through a stream of electroluminescent diodes similar to LED lights, allowing the machine to read the organic composition of each grape. Essentially, it takes a microsecond photo/X-ray that measures the individual berry's color, texture, and organic structure, including shape and density. With the picture of the perfect composite berry "in mind," the optical sorter takes it from there. At a rate of 10,000 frames per second, it compares every single grape to that exact standard, sorting the grapes at a rate of two tons in just 12 minutes. A blast of air blows any grape that doesn't measure up into a separate hopper.

Normally, that amount of grapes would take 15 people an hour to sort through. Of course, those humans wouldn't be able to judge the entirety of the grape the way the optical sorter can. And that can make all the difference. At a cost of $400,000, this optical sorter is wildly expensive, but the quality improvement in the wine is so great that it is worth the expense.

After the fruit has been sorted, the grapes that have passed the test are fed into the stainless steel tanks using the gravity-flow system we talked about earlier. Once the tank has been filled, we add dry ice and allow the grape juice to sit with the skins and seed for at least four to five days. This is known as a cold soak. The cold soak allows the juice to extract the color and tannin gently from the skin in the absence of alcohol, which can accelerate the extraction of hard tannins.

Once a day during the cold soak, we drain off the tank to capture the juice through a screen and then take that juice and put it back into the tank. After the cold soak is complete, the winemakers gradually begin to bring up the temperature in the tanks, finally allowing for yeast fermentation. During this process, yeasts convert the sugar in the juice to alcohol and carbon dioxide. At HALL and WALT, we use natural yeasts (i.e., those that are present on the grapes' skins) and sometimes pure cultured yeasts to carry out the fermentations. This is riskier, but we believe the combination of yeast fermentations provides depth and texture to the wine, along with an additional level of complexity and individuality, and results in a truer expression of terroir.

During fermentation, we will gently punch down the cap in our tanks of Pinot Noir to allow the juice to push through the skins. With Cabernet Sauvignon, we'll do *pump-overs* instead, which means taking the juice that is on the bottom two-thirds of the tank and pumping it into the top of the tank in order to mix the juice.

As we saw with the tank walk, during the fermentation stage, which usually lasts a little more than two weeks, the juice is analyzed for sugar and temperature daily, as well as tasted by our winemakers to monitor the fermentation progress. At the end of that period, some 21 days from the arrival of the grapes to the winery, the majority of the liquid in the tank has turned to wine.

We transfer the free run—the wine we drain through a spigot at the bottom of the tank—into barrels. The remaining gooey, musty content in the tank—including the skins, seeds, and juice—is pressed to extract the residual wine, which amounts to approximately 10 to 15 percent of the volume. Although pressed wine is very common, like most higher-end wineries we use very little—if any—because it tends to be harsh and a bit bitter. Instead, the pressed wine gets sold off as bulk wine that others put their label on. So once again, we're leaving money on the table. Just as we minimize our yield in the vineyard by pruning back the vines and then discarding what doesn't make the final cut on the crush pad, we don't necessarily keep all the wine from each tank. That's part of the cost of making quality wines.

The free run goes into small, 60-gallon oak barrels, with most wines typically being aged in barrels of at least 50 percent new French oak and the remainder in oak barrels no older than two years. We use only French oak and only barrels that are two years old or younger whose grain imparts the more subtle flavors that fit the delicate style and finesse we're aiming for. To save money, we tried experimenting with different barrels, including American, Hungarian, and other types of oak. Then we went right back to French oak. The others just didn't measure up.

We buy from a variety of barrel coopers who source barrels from many different oak forests in France, including Taransaud, Sylvain, Boutes, and Garonnaise for our Cabernet Sauvignons, and Francois Freres (only) for our Pinot Noirs and Chardonnays. Each cooper has its own special technique for the production and seasoning of the barrels, and therefore each producer's barrels have their own distinctive taste profiles. Winemakers approach barrels from different coopers almost as a chef would approach different spices in the making of a special dish, with each having its own flavor characteristics.

At this point, we will inoculate a Chardonnay with malolactic bacteria to encourage malolactic fermentation, and for our reds, allow the malolactic fermentation to occur naturally in the wine. *Malolactic fermentation* is a natural fermentation that converts malic acid (which naturally occurs in grapes) to lactic acid. This conversion reduces the acidity of the wine and makes it more stable for long-term storage and aging. Typically, the malolactic fermentation is complete two to six months following the initial yeast fermentation.

Then we let the barrels rest.

★   ★   ★

The barrels are stored in caves, which provide nearly ideal conditions in terms of temperature control and consistent humidity. Some wineries will add in the additional protection of a cooling system, which is what we did at Rutherford, but this is largely unnecessary. The goal is to store the wine at 55 degrees Fahrenheit and at 68 percent relative humidity to minimize evaporation, also known as *angel's share*. Even so, we have to top off the barrels regularly. Thirsty little angel!

We used to periodically rack the Cabernet Sauvignons during this barrel aging period to clarify them and help them evolve. The idea was that while the wine ages, the *lees* (the dead yeast and other particles) fall to the bottom of the barrel. *Racking,* a traditional approach that was started in Bordeaux, uses gravity to pour the clear wine off the top of the barrel into another barrel, leaving the sediment behind.

The majority of winemakers rack their wines, usually quarterly, because that's what they do in Bordeaux. But Bordeaux's Cabernet Sauvignons are much different than ours. For starters, they're less ripe. They're also more austere, more astringent, and they have more tannin, all of which can be corrected through racking since the oxygen that's introduced will help soften tannins. But too much oxygen destroys freshness and depletes color, personality, fragrance, and nuance. According to Steve, if you get your tannins right through all the meticulous work you've done on a shoot-by-shoot, cluster-by-cluster basis in the vineyard, and you've gotten everything right on the crush pad and during fermentation, then your tannins should be perfectly fine. Plus, since we don't add pressed wine, which would add dirt and particulate matter, we don't need to rack for clarity. So why rack?

Our Cabernet Sauvignons sit in the barrels for anywhere from 18 to 24 months, compared to 10 to 12 months for the Pinot Noirs. (The exact length of time depends on both the wine and the vineyard.) This allows the wines to develop and integrate the flavors of the oak. Then it's time to blend.

Blending is like using a huge chemistry set. Sometimes we have literally hundreds of test tubes full of different pure wine samples. Most blending sessions start at 7:30 a.m. because that's when one's palate is the freshest, so the wines are tasted in their purest and most intense manner at the beginning of the day. Winemakers don't just drink on the job, they drink wine for breakfast—whether they like it or not.

To those not involved in the wine business, spending a day tasting and blending wines sounds more like entertainment than work. In reality, these are long, stressful, exhausting, and downright critical days.

Steve, Megan, and Alison taste every single fermentation lot, each of which reflects a separate vineyard block. Within fermentation lots, they might even taste individual barrels. Barrels are not perfectly consistent entities since they come from wood that's been aged in a yard for three years. Those variations between barrels impact the taste of the wine, so when we're making our very top-of-the-line wines, we'll take the very, very best barrels from individual lots to create our best blends.

All this translates to a lot of tasting, since we have more than 220 Cabernet Sauvignon lots as of this writing. By noon, everybody's teeth have turned purple. Our winemakers start out by evaluating each individual lot to assess quality. Not all the wine that has been aged in the barrels gets used. Any wine deemed inadequate after the tastings, for whatever reason, is sold to the bulk wine market. Once again, that costs us, since we wind up getting about $20 a gallon, instead of the $55 *a bottle* we would get for our Napa Cabernet Sauvignon.

After Steve and his team have culled out the substandard wine, they start discussing each lot. They grade each one, and jot down notes on huge tasting sheets about how the wines taste, what they taste like, and what's notable about them. Then they start to blend, taking more notes in the process. They work on blending our most important wines, such as Exzellenz, first. Since Exzellenz comes 100 percent from our Sacrashe vineyard, they'll taste all 20 of the Sacrashe lots, assessing each. At this point they're trying to determine which of the best lots have the best components. Once the best lots are determined, individual barrels within these lots are evaluated. The team reviews potential blends before trying to put together a few. Steve makes the ultimate decision, but having multiple palates and a team with a very calibrated approach to winemaking is invaluable.

With other wines they'll blend from two or three different lots to try to create harmony or interest or balance. They might start with three different components, one that constitutes 80 percent of the blend, let's say, and the other two making up the remaining 20 percent in varying ratios. By the time Steve and his team are finalizing the blend, they'll try tweaking those ratios by as little as half a percent. Then, as always, they do a blind tasting and compare it to the current favorite.

Blending happens after the wines have been in barrels for some six to nine months, and a secondary fermentation has taken place. After the winemakers have nailed all their blends in the tiny beakers they're using, the wines are actually blended in the winery and then returned to barrels where they'll spend another 12 to 18 months before being bottled.

The shape of the bottle is determined by the type of wine. Wines like Cabernet Sauvignon and Sauvignon Blanc that originated in France's Bordeaux will have a bottle with high, distinct shoulders to help catch the sediment. Wines like Pinot Noir and Chardonnay that stem from the Burgundy region have bottles with wider bases and sloping shoulders.

Once the wine is bottled, we typically allow the wines to age for an additional six to twelve months in the bottle before releasing them for consumption. This additional aging allows the wines to further develop, soften, and evolve to the delicious and complex style that is a trademark of HALL and WALT wines. Many of our wines will continue to develop and improve with additional years of cellar aging.

Finally, three years after harvest, our Cabernet Sauvignon is ready to be released. And while tradition and technology have both played a role in its inception, the winemaker's artistry is what makes or breaks this product that's been so long in the making. In short, the winemaker is key to the winery. That's why we were so lucky to wind up with Steve. Not only is this Napa Valley native uber-precise and over-the-top finicky when it comes to detail, he has a remarkable palate which comes through in the wines he crafts. He also combines a super technical approach to winemaking with a very of-the-land approach. Some winemakers spend very little time in the vineyard. Not Steve. He's all about the vineyard and how it grows. As we've said, he and Don Munk, our vineyard manager, often wander through the grapevines together. Finally, in addition to being really hardworking, we love that Steve is a risk taker.

Taking creative risks constitutes a big part of going the extra mile when it comes to making great wines. Last year, for example, Steve began to wonder if some of the terroir qualities reflected in Pinot Noirs are actually imparted from the soil itself. So he threw some of the dirt from Rita's Crown vineyard, located in the Santa Barbara County's Santa Rita region, into grapes from a vineyard in Northern California's Russian River Valley. He wanted to see if that Southern California dirt could impact the overall flavor and aroma profile of the Russian River Valley Pinot Noir.

Some people would have thought that was crazy, but we love the result. In blind tastings, the presence of that earthy, dusty, mineral character that distinctly comes from the windswept Santa Barbara vineyard with its sedimentary, calcareous soil had clearly been transmitted to the grapes from the vineyard in the Russian River Valley. Steve liked the results so much that he added in even more dirt the next time around.

Steve also adds grape stems to our Pinot Noir juice while it's fermenting. Knowing that the stems, which can impart a lovely paprika note, can also impart green, harsh, bitter tannins, especially once they've gotten mangled and cracked after going through the destemmer, Steve came up with the idea of slowly roasting them. The heat, he knew, would denature the really aggressive tannins. So for our WALT Pinot Noirs, we'll rinse off all the sugars from the stems and then put them in a chili roaster. Very slowly and lightly so as not to pick up any charry or smoky flavors, we'll heat them before throwing them into the fermentation tanks.

KATHRYN

We set aside many lots each harvest to test new techniques. I especially love this part of Steve's work. He is always pushing the envelope and looking for nuance. Sometimes the test is obvious, like the impact of open tank versus closed tank fermentation. Sometimes it is beautifully subtle. Do we drain juice off leaving 90 percent of the original juice to soak on the skins or do we leave 85 percent of the juice on to soak? Which will make a better wine? We don't know so we run experiments to see. We think the more concentrated juice, the one with 15 percent drained off, will give us more intense flavors, but that's not clear. That's why this is an art. And there's gratefully not one machine in the land that can give us the answer. It's a decision made through the beautiful interplay of the human senses.

Since there is no one way to make great wine, we do these kinds of experiments as part of research and development. Every year we try something new. As a result, a lot of our wine—and our success—is driven by trial and error. Sometime we mess up and bulk out the wine. But often the risks and experiments result in wines that are very special.

We also know that striving for top quality means we will have to bulk sale a higher than typical amount of our wine.

So while a ton of grapes generally makes about 60 or 63 cases of red wine, in our case it makes only about 50. As in the fields, our production is oriented toward quality versus quantity. Just as our farming techniques increase the cost of growing our grapes, this dramatically increases the cost of making our wine, but it's worth it. Our internal saying is: *No shortcuts—no excuses!*

Winemaking, however, is not a solo operation. It's one of the few activities that's better done by committee. So while you need somebody who makes the final decision, having a stellar team is critical when it comes to making stellar wine. We've been fortunate to be able to tap the talents of our WALT winemaker Megan Gunderson. She and Steve have now been working together for so long that during harvest, when there's so much work happening so fast that it seems like a blur, Steve will say, "I think we need to" and Megan will complete his sentence with, "...turn it up two degrees and leave it there for two hours." They, along with Alison Frichtl, have chemistry when it comes time for tasting and blending, which makes them such a wonderful team.

We know that a lot of the results we've gotten—including winding up with such all-star winemakers—are due to luck. We also know that if you keep trying new things and keep high standards, you put yourself in a position to get lucky.

CHAPTER 22

The Quest for Perfection

Kathryn's favorite T-shirt reads: *Life is too short to drink bad wine.* And it's too short to spend your time in a business that doesn't give you a thrill. We've had more than our share of thrills thanks to the wines we produce and the people we've met along the way.

Wine is different, and wine experiences, as we've noted before, often trigger lasting positive memories. We realized just how far that impact reaches over dinner during an educational trip to Israel sponsored by the World Presidents' Organization. The local hosts from Israel's chapter had taken about a hundred of us—all presidents of companies from around the world and their spouses—on a late afternoon hike in the desert. After about an hour, just as it was starting to get a little dark, we turned the corner to find a feast awaiting. In the midst of a vineyard, local dishes and wine abounded on long tables adorned with glasses, candles, and grape clusters strewn down the middle.

We sat next to a couple from Japan and tried to make

conversation. The wife spoke just a little English; her husband spoke even less. Since we speak no Japanese, we knew it was not going to be easy. So we stuck with the basics.

"Where are you from?" we asked.

"Japan."

"Where are you from?" they asked. "What do you do?"

"Napa Valley. We make wine."

All of a sudden the Japanese gentleman exclaimed, "Chandelier!"

"What?" we asked.

"Chandelier," he repeated, his voice choked with emotion. "Chandelier."

Then, in very broken English, he explained that he had been to this underground winery that has a beautiful chandelier. When we said it was ours, he was beyond excited.

As wonderful as it is to see people respond to our chandelier or other art, it's the wine that excites most people.

"Your Merlot changed my life," a woman told Craig when he was shopping for a Valentine's gift for Kathryn a few years ago.

More recently, we were at a lobster and Pinot Noir picnic for 146 of our wine club members at Bob's Ranch, a new vineyard we bought in Sonoma and named after Kathryn's father. That day, both of us heard kind stories about how people came to enjoy WALT and/or HALL wines and how deeply they felt about their experiences. No financial results could impart a greater sense of pride.

That's what it's all about. If technology allows us to share that kind of high-end wine experience with huge numbers of people, how wonderful is that? This business is not about selling the most wine. It's not about selling the most expensive wine. It's about selling terrific, high-quality wine at a good value and encouraging as many people as possible to enjoy it. Helping wine aficionados discover the type of wine they like (having offered the best possible value), and then supporting the way in which they enjoy it—that's our future.

We love that people often come up to us in random places, introduce themselves, and thank us for our winery and, more importantly, our wine and their experiences with it, describing exactly where they were, what they were doing, and how the wine tasted. We do the same with each other. As we write, we think about a warm sunny afternoon last month, having lunch and wine at a beautiful family-owned, historic winery in Bolgheri, Italy. We sat at lunch with one of the family members, lush, green vineyards on every side, and listened to her share how her multi-generational heritage in the wine business creates a feeling of responsibility to those who went before, but even more to those family members who will follow. The long, smoky finish of the wine we drank will remain as much of a memory as the graciousness of our hostess and the beauty of the setting.

Hearing and sharing these wine experiences just never gets old. It's truly an honor to be involved with something that captures life in a bottle. Of course, having people rave about our wines is pretty great as well.

HALL and WALT wines have been the beneficiaries of some very high critical scores. As we write, just counting four great critics, HALL has been awarded more than 261 scores of 90 points or above, and WALT, which has been in existence for under four years, has received 61.

During the past 12 years, there were many wines that we thought deserved a high score that didn't make it, and, honestly, one that we thought didn't warrant it (we'll never tell which). The score is only the icing, not the cake, but we love the affirmation that we're doing well. We love the boost in sales and the heightened visibility for our brand. And we love the fact that the visibility we've gained within the industry because of our strong scores allows us to buy grapes from top vineyards that wouldn't otherwise sell to us.

CRAIG

Our number of over-90-point scores changes so fast that it reminds me of growing up in the Midwest and seeing the McDonald's signs showing the number of hamburgers sold change almost every day. While I don't take that for granted, I must admit every high score is just one more nice thing, but not anything to dwell on. We simply move on and try to get better and better, never resting on the laurels of any critical praise.

From the beginning, we've strived to make the most perfect wine possible. For us, perfection is defined as a wine that, from our vineyard through to the winemaking, achieves its full potential.

In January 2013, that quest for perfection inspired our winemaker Steve Leveque to put together a research-oriented focus group called 100-Point Wine. The goal of the group, which consisted of Steve, our vineyard manager Don Munk, and high-end consulting viticulturists, was to explore every possibility—especially any new viticulture practices, wine-making techniques, and hunches—that could lead to our creating a 100-point wine. Little did we know that we'd already pulled that off, and with a vintage that many wine critics had written off.

Usually when one of our wines surpasses the others, it's because with that particular wine the gods smiled in our favor, allowing our vineyard manager and our winemakers to take full advantage of a perfect growing season and perfect terroir. That wasn't the case in 2010. That year, according to *Wine Spectator,* "Much of California faced a brutal growing season as a cool, gray summer gave way to blistering heat waves, followed by torrential rains."

Due to the colder than usual temperatures at the beginning of the growing season, the grapes matured more slowly than usual. Late in the season we pulled leaves because we knew the summer heat was over and we still needed the grapes' tannins to develop. Opening up the canopy would allow more sunlight in. Then news hit that a monster storm was tracking from Japan to the West Coast. Each passing day during the lead-up to the storm brought more certainty that a large amount of rain would drench the North Coast.

Steve called Mike Reynolds.

"I know you're traveling, but I wanted you to know that the weather forecast is worse than expected," he told our president. "I was in the vineyard today, and the grapes are just not ripe. We plan to let the grapes hang through the rain."

The late-season rains could compromise all the grapes in that section of our prized Sacrashe vineyard in not just one but several ways. For starters, during the fall we don't irrigate much and usually haven't irrigated for a while. Because it's not that hot, the vine doesn't really need water. So any water it gets, say from a rainstorm, will actually go straight to the berries, thereby reducing or diluting the sugar that's in the grapes. That would be bad enough, but big rain events, especially at the final end of the season, can also lead to mold, rot, and mildew, which can send the grapes sideways and negatively impact the flavors, texture, or color in the wine. Deciding not to pick before a rainstorm of this size would also mean that we wouldn't be able to harvest for another few days because the tractors wouldn't be able to get through the mud, which would compound the risk.

"I agree. If the grapes are not ripe, then we can't pick," Mike responded, even though most Napa growers were scrambling to harvest their grapes before the storm hit. "Do the best you can. Good thing we purchased the optical sorter this year. We're going to need it."

As a general rule, we try to process the grapes, which means sorting, destemming, and crushing them and then getting the juice to the tank, within 24 hours from when the grapes are harvested. The optical sorter not only helped us meet that timeline that season, it ensured that none of the grapes that had been adversely impacted by the rain made it into the fermentation tank. Investing in that optical sorter had been a financial risk, just as leaving the grapes on the vine had been a financial risk, but that's always been our style. Go big or go home. That approach can be scary, but when it works as well as it did in 2010, the payoff is huge. Of course, we wouldn't know just how well our risk taking had panned out until three years later. At the time, we were just focused on how to mitigate the impact of the season's cold weather.

A cold year is going to give you harder tannin, especially when it comes to the seeds, so our winemakers delib-erately changed our typical fermentation approach to avoid over-extracting the seed tannin. The first 10 to 14 days of fermentation is when we really create the wine since the leverage that you have as a winemaker to change the style and quality of the wine once it's barreled is minimal. In 2010, we had to balance our desire to create a big, rich, dense wine, which means giving it plenty of contact with the grape skins and seeds, with the harshness of that year's under-ripe seed tannins. So Steve chose to increase the cold-soak period, a gentler way of extracting tannins that would help him keep the seed extraction to a minimum. He followed that with fewer than normal and shorter than normal pump-overs, the process of transferring the fermenting juice to a storage tank and then splashing it back in over the *cap* (the grape skins, seeds, and pulp) that floats at the top of the fermentation tank. He also exposed the juice to more oxygen than usual in order to mitigate the harshness from the seed tannin.

Oddly enough, despite all the weather-related challenges, once we tasted the wines in 2013, we all thought that the 2010 vintage was stronger than the prior year's. The wines were richer and had more tannin. But just because we liked them didn't mean that the critics would, especially since early industry reviews of the 2010 vintage as a whole were mixed. So while we didn't expect the worst when we sent in our wines to be reviewed, we certainly didn't expect the best.

We got our first hint that things were looking good during the third week of October 2013, about a week before the annual Robert Parker reviews were due out. At the *Wine*

Spectator event held at the Marriott Marquis in New York, David Ramey came over to taste the HALL and WALT wines Mike Reynolds was pouring. After exchanging pleasantries, David, who had worked for us as a consultant in the early days, mentioned that he had some interesting news to share.

"I tasted wines at my winery with Robert Parker, who is aware of our past connection," he said to Mike. "He told me that the 2010 HALL wines he tasted were very impressive."

David punctuated his statement with a smile. "That's a good sign," he concluded.

Boy was he right!

On November 3, 2013, Steve got into work early. He knew Robert Parker's scores were being released that day. Feeling a bit like a zombie after months of working the harvest without a break, he checked the Robert Parker website where he found a number of big scores for our wines. Then he saw that Parker had awarded us a 100-point score for our 2010 HALL Exzellenz Cabernet Sauvignon.

That's odd, he thought to himself. *I think that says a hundred points. That can't be.*

He picked up the phone and called Mike straightaway. "Go onto the Parker website and see what the hell our scores are," Steve said. "Because I think we got 100."

"What?" Mike stammered.

"Just do it and let me know if it's true," Steve answered.

It was true.

Kathryn learned of the perfect score at 9:30 that same morning as she was driving into San Francisco. The emotions flooding through her were so strong that she would have—and probably should have—pulled off the road had that been possible.

KATHRYN

Most mornings when I wake up in our home on the Sacrashe vineyard, I reflect on how lucky I am to be living this life with Craig, growing grapes as my parents did, and making and sharing wine with wonderful people. I just can't refer to this as work. This is living a dream. But my dream had not anticipated the thrill of the letter from Robert Parker.

"I wanted you to be one of the first to have a copy of the newest *Wine Advocate,* which includes the 2013 Napa report," read the letter Robert Parker wrote to Kathryn. "I hope you enjoy the reviews of your wines. I certainly enjoyed tasting them. Keep up the good work."

So few have been lucky enough to earn a perfect score of 100. Two weeks after we got the news, Naoka Dalla Valle, who received a perfect score from Robert Parker in 1995 for her 1992 vintage and another for the 1993 vintage the following year, welcomed us into this elite club with a lovely note of congratulations. Although her winery, Dalla Valle Vineyards, is located in Oakville about ten minutes from our St. Helena facility, she had been in Hong Kong when she wrote us. News of a perfect score travels fast in our community.

The whole thing was a heady experience. We'd be lying if we said otherwise. But we also know that while a wine may achieve a perfect score, there is no such thing as a perfect wine.

A perfect score implies that there's an end to the whole experience or whole project. In this world of wine, there's never an end. There's just the constant quest for perfection, as elusive as that may be. Besides, the real perfect score comes not from a critic but from the person who has enjoyed our wine and returns for more.

This singularly unique wine business is all about trying to make the very best wine possible while providing an environment that encourages wine to be an enjoyable experience for people as they go about their lives. Just like wine, the wine business is a living, changing organism that continues to morph. But while the way one farms grapes, the way one makes wine, and the way one markets it are all evolving, one thing remains constant: the thrill of experiencing a memorable Cabernet Sauvignon, Pinot Noir, Merlot, Chardonnay, Sauvignon Blanc, and more.

Kathryn's love for wine got us into this business, a love Craig now shares.

CRAIG

Kathryn's passion and high energy level set the pace and spirit for the soul of our wine business. Where I may have come in was to set a bit of the cultural value that helped us in 2010 in the area of empowerment and risk. Kathryn shares my view that we pick people and then encourage them to try new things and take chances. Most importantly, we empower them to make decisions and do their jobs. To us that's just common sense, but we hear that it's unusual not just in the wine business, but in our other businesses as well. Lots of other companies seem to be more regimented and run in a way that makes people afraid to do what they believe is right.

We're okay with people making mistakes as long as those mistakes don't get repeated. What we are not okay with is people taking too much of a risk-averse path. If we had not taken risks in 2010, we wouldn't have come through with a really good wine.

We know that a perfect score is far from a perfect wine, and we will never really get to where we have a perfect wine. That said, we love trying. We also love to see how our team feels fully ready, willing, and able to do the very best they can and make decisions that sometimes will result in the payoff we had with the 2010 Exzellenz.

At the core of our two wine brands are the heart, soul, and talents of our risk-taking winemaking team—Steve, Megan, and Alison—along with their cellar crew. But so many other talented people in other areas—hospitality, finance, marketing, phones and email, wine clubs, wholesale sales—make it all happen every day. Plus we have the ongoing guidance of our advisory board members who share their expertise from their respective fields—distribution, hospitality, public relations, media, and IT—so we feel surrounded by talented folks who have our back. As detailed in our Acknowledgments, these individuals have really provided us with critical perspective.

Making and selling great wine is a long-term process that involves this entire team. Every six months, almost from the start, we've held multi-day planning meetings during which we analyze each area of operation. Having created an annual budget and business plan, we look at where we are compared to where we had hoped to be. We also hold town hall meetings with our employees and encourage questions, open dialogue, and sharing ideas across departments.

Not counting Mike Reynolds and ourselves, four members of our team have been here more than ten years. Natalie Bell, who started in January 2003 right after Mike came aboard, is now Mike's assistant and our universally loved and approachable human resources director for both HALL and WALT Wines. Celfo Guzman, a multi-talented cellar worker, started with us in August 2005 and worked Rutherford winery's first harvest. Richard Reeves, based in Tampa, has become the face of HALL and WALT in the Southeast region. As WALT general manager and former director of membership, Jeff Zappelli has built loyal wine clubs for HALL and WALT literally from the ground up, traveling across the country holding wine dinners at members' homes.

Most of these folks were here when we were meeting in our dining room—partly because we didn't have another place to meet and partly because we could. Of course, some of our newer arrivals have also dramatically impacted our brand and our direction. Our digital presence has taken a wonderful new turn thanks to Emily Harrison, our director of marketing, who joined us in January 2015. Emily led the redesign of our websites and forges new ground for us in e-commerce and social media with her ever-growing team of creatives and techies.

No one in our remarkable team has been more central over the years to WALT and HALL than Mike Reynolds. He simply knows how to do everything, from cleaning out a tank to running a board meeting, from making wine to marketing and selling it. He manages to rise to every challenge no matter how daunting. Plus, he can seamlessly deal with, and often mediate between, the two of us. Mike has been an invaluable guide, support, and leader, and has been absolutely key in building the winery brands.

KATHRYN

Years ago, I was interviewed by a reporter from a prominent wine magazine. I was telling him about how much I loved the business and looked forward to developing a long-term, serious brand. He asked why he should believe me.

"So many people from outside the Valley who have been successful in other non-wine-related endeavors come here with the stated intention of building a brand, but it's really only a hobby," he said. "Prove that you're serious."

How do you respond to that? I understood his point. It's easy to talk about passion and intention and commitment. It is also easy to talk about how great a wine is. But until you see, smell, swirl, taste it, you won't know.

I knew we were serious. Plus Craig and I are both very determined people. I told him that all I had was my experience, background, and intention, but in a few years he would see that we were going to make a difference in the industry.

We hope we can make a difference. It's a work in progress, and we're committed to using every advantage we can, including technology, to do this. Together with our talented, hardworking, and passionate team, we intend to continue to grow a wine business that makes us all proud.

A big part of that has to do with the personal connection we have with our guests. If you come to visit our St. Helena winery, we want you to have fun. The visit to the winery should be informative and relaxing. You'll experience the juxtaposition of history with the modern art and architecture we love. You'll experience the latest winemaking technology. And you'll experience some great wines.

As we look to the future, we hope that our wines continue to be a part of the memorable happenings in our customers' lives—with good friends and family, in Napa or across the country or around the world—as it is our experience that food and wine have a way of bringing people together.

We certainly didn't start out with these goals. To be honest, we had no idea what we were getting into when we started this venture. But boy do we love it.

Bringing this down to the most basic, the best thing about making wine is that it allows us to share what we love about being part of Napa Valley. This free and easy Napa lifestyle is very much a part of our brand and a part of our lives. May we never forget that.

Fortunately, for Kathryn, Napa has become as familiar and comfortable as Mendocino ever was. As for Craig, he now *really* knows rosé is not red and white wine mixed together.

We'll drink to that.

ACKNOWLEDGMENTS

One of the greatest joys in writing this book is the chance to thank those who have been a part of our twenty-year Napa journey and who have more recently helped us in our role as authors. The list of folks to thank starts with everyone over the years who has been a part of the HALL and WALT teams. Every person on the team has contributed to making our shared dreams a reality. We have learned and grown from you all.

No one on this team has been as critical as our winery president, Mike Reynolds, who has taught us more about the wine business than we ever knew to question. His commitment to excellence in our wines and to the excellence of the team that makes, markets, and sells them has been at the core of our growth and success. He works hard and he does so many things well. Except for one thing: He will not take his due credit. Mike makes everyone around him stronger, and always downplays his own efforts. As in all we do at the winery, Mike continued to play a central role in the writing, editing, and strategy of this book. Thank you, Mike. You know how critical you are to everything HALL and WALT, even if you won't say it. But we will.

Natalie Bell, our nurturing human resources manager and right hand to Mike, provided key editing and advice on content. Jeff Zappelli, as one of our most tenured team members, has been a trusted resource for facts we couldn't recall. You have done a fantastic job at HALL over the years, Jeff, and we are excited to see you now put your enthusiasm and talent into building WALT in your new role as general manager. Our entire marketing team, led by Emily Harrison, stepped up on every occasion—and of that terrific team no one has been more key than Justine Di Fede, whose beautiful photography not only visually defines our brands to the public, but also graces the color insert of this book. Justine, you are a delight to work with and a great talent.

You must do everything right in this business, but great wine is the *sine qua non* of the equation. Without the talent and dedication of our production team, we would not be writing about a 100-point wine or producing the many other wines of which we are so proud. Don Munk—a native Napan whose personal contacts have been a huge part of our ability to partner with some of the Valley's greatest vineyard owners—and his team work tirelessly to find the best possible vineyards and to support farming techniques that take full advantage of what they find. WALT winemaker/ associate HALL winemaker Megan Gunderson and assistant winemaker Allison Frichtl bring awesome palates, talent, and leadership to our winemaking effort and manage a dedicated, hardworking cellar team.

Our amazing, risk-taking director of winemaking, Steve Leveque, who leads this whole production team, continually pushes the envelope to explore ways to improve the wines we make. Steve, your pursuit of perfection pushes us all to do better. Thank you for your leadership and genius as well as the extensive input you provided to this book.

To our vineyard partners, thank you for putting your trust and your amazing grapes in our care. Without great grapes at the start, there is no hope of producing great wine. We are awed by your commitment to quality.

Our advisory board, Wayne Wright, Lee Schepps, Susan Butenhoff, Tom Carrol, Mike Bell, Don Braun, and former members Bob Long, Larry Levey, and Michael Jenkins, have given us critical counsel over the years. Thank you for your talent, generosity, and for continuing to tell us things we don't want, but need to hear.

Thank you to our partners, who have become our strongest ambassadors and whose investment during a critical financial period enabled us to complete the St. Helena winery. The degree to which your sales efforts in restaurants all over the country have expanded our presence and brand far exceeds our expectation.

This book would not have happened without our agents and friends Jan Miller, owner and founder of Dupree Miller, and her associate, Nena Madonia Oshman. They have guided us every step in this process and led us to the best team of publishers any author could envision. To Rolf Zettersten and Joey Paul of Hachette, thank you for your encouragement, patience, and guidance. And we are thrilled that you enjoy our wines.

Thank you to our distributors who have beaten the pavement, calling on restaurants and stores across the country telling our story and sharing our wines in ways far beyond our capacity to do so. You have helped us build our brands and without your efforts we could never have grown at the pace we have.

To our Napa friends and fellow vintners, thank you for your counsel and friendship. We are very lucky to share this amazing valley with you.

We love to write, but we needed help. In Linden Gross we found not only a wordsmith, but also a strategist, creative partner, editor, and part-time marriage counselor who could mediate tactfully between us. Thank you, Linden, for going the extra mile from the first step to the last. You are the best.

Thank you to our four wonderful children starting with Jet and her husband, Parker, and their children, PJ and Ellie; our daughter Independence and her children, Sebastian and Maximilian; our son, David; and our daughter Jennifer and her husband, Eric. Your encouragement, feedback, and patience in hearing this story told repeatedly for a year and a half and each time reacting as if it were fresh could only have come from the heart. Everything pales in comparison to the support we feel from your love.

Finally, thank you to our club members and to everyone who enjoys our wines and our wineries. Without you, there would be no wine, no book, no chandelier, and no Bunny Foo Foo.

A GLOSSARY OF TERMS, HALL-STYLE

Angel's share—Wine that evaporates and goes to "wine heaven" while aging in barrels. This is wine that is lost to evaporation as it ages in barrels.

Automated P.O. trial—When the winemaker conducts too many research trials, so that his staff automatically gets pissed off. *P.O.* also refers to a dedicated pump and equipment being used to automatically *pump over* a tank during fermentation. We are conducting a trial to evaluate the quality of this automation.

Basket press—Can turn your interns into basket cases. A press that only holds small amounts of pomace (see definition on page 205) at a time, but that is gentler so the resulting quality is higher. The pomace is added to a large metal basket and a pneumatic arm pushes down and squeezes the wine out of the sides of the basket. The interns go crazy when they have to dig out the pomace once it's been pressed and put it in the bladder press for the final squeeze.

Bloom—Magic. Reproduction at its finest, when the flowers on the grapevines begin to make berries.

Brix—Where to go in the Napa Valley for a great Happy Hour (just north of Yountville on Highway 29). Also, the sugar content of grapes and wine, which in the U.S. is measured by a system called the Brix scale. The Brix is determined by a hydrometer, which indicates a liquid's specific gravity (the density of a liquid in relation to that of pure water). Each degree Brix is equivalent to 1 gram of sugar per 100 grams of grape juice. The grapes for most table wines have a Brix reading of 22 to 26 degrees at harvest.

Bud break—No, this is not when we take a break to drink Bud or indulge in that other substance that grows in Mendocino. Bud break is when the soil warms up and the vine sends a hormonal signal to the plant to wake up and start growing.

Bung—Yes, bung not burn. Bung is the stopper that goes on the top of the barrel.

Cellar rat—A four-legged, short animal in a basement or cellar. Well, not really. How about: a two-legged intern or full-time employee who makes sure the wine is being properly treated after fermentation (i.e., during pump-overs and all those fun things) per the winemaker's instructions. Cellar rats are lower-level employees who hopefully learn, grow, and become big-time winemakers, and who then tell new cellar rats what to do.

Crop estimations—This is what Craig asks Don, Mike, and Steve about almost daily every summer as we get close to harvest. He wants them to figure out how much fruit we will be bringing to the winery during harvest. The estimations are usually within +/- 100 percent of actual. The truth is crop estimates are important and generally can be accurate within a 2- or 3-percent margin.

Free run—Twice annually, Napa hosts a 5K run through the vineyards, and no admission fees are required. Well, not really. More truthfully and more pertinent to wine, free run is the wine that freely drains from a red fermentation tank (and no, the tank isn't red, it's just full of red wine). What's left in the tank is squeezed out of the pomace—the pressed wine. The free run is the higher-quality portion—we sell almost all of our pressed wine to other wineries in Napa.

HALL Pass—A teacher's note letting a student leave a class when nature calls. Or a free wine-tasting card for members at HALL or WALT, also good for a natural calling—enjoying great wine and great experiences.

Interns—Also referred to as power-wash slaves. These are paid seasonal workers at the bottom of the winemaking totem pole. The most talented ones can party all night and come in and work a 14-hour shift of hard labor the next day.

Malolactic—This is a funny-sounding, geeky wine word that will make for great conversation on a first date—i.e., "Do you think that Chardonnay underwent malolactic?" It is actually about bacterial fermentation that converts malic acid in wine (the same acid present in green apples) to lactic acid (the acid in cream and milk). Also referred to as *ml,* this process happens naturally in red wines; with whites the winemaker chooses whether to perform malolactic. Our WALT Chardonnay undergoes full malolactic, while our HALL Sauvignon Blanc is not permitted to undergo malolactic at all.

Napa—The name the Native Americans gave to the beautiful valley that we and others share and enjoy so much. Also a world-famous region for making—and drinking—high-quality wine (particularly Cabernet Sauvignon).

No shortcuts, no excuses—The internal model of the HALL winemaking team in their quest for Exzellenz and excellence.

Oak barrels—An extremely expensive spice rack—aka a magical 60-gallon French oak container—that allows us to store the wine for aging. The oak adds structure and richness to the wine, as well as a unique spicy aromatic bouquet that delivers complexity and nuance to each bottle.

Passes—Frequent bar activity between the sexes. Also the term we use to describe when a crew is working in our vineyards, performing any type of viticultural activity.

Pomace—How ladies (or men) keep their heels clean and smooth for stomping those grapes. Oops, actually that's *pumice,* but close enough. In reality, pomace is the compacted skins and seeds that are removed from the bladder or basket press after squeezing to capture the pressed portion of the wines.

Pressed wine—Not to be confused with promotional wine given to local journalists to garner good press. This is wine left over after the free run wine has left the building (er, barrel). It's made from the grapes being smushed together in a wine press.

Pump-over—What our interns do for hours on end September through November, as opposed to *pumped up,* which we all are just before the grapes come in. Also known as *remontage,* it is the process of pumping red wine up from the bottom of the tank and splashing it over the top of the fermenting must to extract color and flavor.

RFBs—See YFBs on page 207 for an explanation. The ones we use are red—"the HALL red"—and they're just as aggravating as the yellow ones.

Scorpion—Found on the backs of your coworkers when working with barrels in caves. Not really. Actually, the trademark name of technology used by ETS Laboratories in St. Helena to quantify wine-specific strains of yeast and bacteria.

Set—The end of a round in tennis. Oops, wrong *set.* In this case, it's the period when—if bloom was a success—the flowers on the grapevine that have self-pollinated begin to mature into berries.

Suckering—Something that gentlemen (or women) vintners can do on weekends. Vines are like weeds. If they aren't properly managed they will grow everywhere. Suckering is the act of removing unwanted growth from the trunks and cordons of the vines so they grow the way we want them to. Too bad we can't do that with our children. Usually we sucker in early spring just after bud break.

Thief—Someone you don't ever want working for you or, in the wine context, a foot-plus-long glass tube. You put one end into a barrel of wine and suck on the other just enough for wine to come into the tube. Then you put your thumb over the end you sucked on, lift the tube out of the barrel and "barrel taste" the wine.

UV tank sanitation—A tanning bed for our tanks. Or cutting-edge technology that uses UV light to sterilize stainless steel tanks. This can save thousands of gallons of water (especially important during a drought) as well as thousands of dollars in cleaning agents.

Veraison—A funny word the French invented to complicate winemaking if you don't speak French. It is the catalyst for harvest. We use the term to describe the onset of ripening in a vineyard. Red grapes form color during veraison, and all grapes become soft and start to accumulate sugar and flavors.

YFBs—An acronym for those annoyingly small, yellow bins used to collect grapes during harvest. A term not to be used in front of your grandmother, who will be sure to ask you what the *F* stands for.